LED ZEPPELIN

Barney Hoskyns

RODALE

This is one for my great friend and fellow
Zephead Tom Butler

Rodale books may be purchased for business or promotional use
or for special sales. For information, please write to:

Special Markets Department, Rodale Inc., 733 Third Avenue,
New York, NY 10017

Printed in the United States of America
Rodale Inc. makes every effort to use acid-free ∞,
recycled paper ♻.

Book design by Drew Frantzen

Library of Congress Cataloging-in-Publication Data
Hoskyns, Barney.
    Led Zeppelin IV / Barney Hoskyns.
        p.   cm.
    ISBN-13 978–1–59486–370–7 hardcover
    ISBN-10 1–59486–370–9 hardcover
    1. Led Zeppelin (Musical group) 2. Led Zeppelin (Musical
group). Led Zeppelin IV. 3. Rock music—1971-1980—History
and criticism. I. Title.
    ML421.L4H67 2006
    782.42166092'2—dc22   2006024050

Distributed to the book trade by Holtzbrinck Publishers

2 4 6 8 10 9 7 5 3 1 hardcover

CONTENTS

ACKNOWLEDGMENTS

MY THANKS to Robert Plant, Jimmy Page, and John Paul Jones for interviews conducted in 2003. Also to Richard Cole, Henry Smith, Jack White, Pamela Des Barres, Nick Kent, and Nancy Retchin.

The book would not have been possible without the work or help of Dave (*Tight But Loose*) Lewis or my agent, Sarah Lazin. Finally, my gratitude goes to Pete Fornatale, who commissioned the book and was supportive and sensitive throughout its writing.

INTRODUCTION
HOW YEARS AGO IN DAYS OF OLD...

EVEN NOW, after all these years of big-hair wannabes, "Get the Led Out" stoners, and idiot tribute bands, there's something so fierce and coruscating about Led Zeppelin in their prime that it can scare you half to death.

Watching the live 1970 footage of the group on 2003's *DVD*, I was reminded of my first pubescent exposure to these four horsemen of the rock apocalypse, with their strangulated shrieking, their blood-curdling riffology, their serpentine tendrils of hair. I saw all too clearly why the marauding quartet of Jimmy Page, Robert Plant, John Paul Jones, and John "Bonzo" Bonham was so terrifyingly off-limits to callow teenyboppers such as myself. (My buddy John Smeddle had a

1

Robert Plant poster on the dormitory wall, but my buddy John Smeddle had an Older Brother. And Led Zeppelin was nothing if not Older Brothers' Rock.)

When my glam-rock passions flagged circa 1973, what stood lean and mean over Marc Bolan's ruin was the savage sensuality of those first four Zeppelin albums: the grinding menace of "Dazed and Confused," the bestial lustfest that was "Whole Lotta Love," the searing anguish of "Since I've Been Loving You," and the primordial blues-funk bonequake that powered "When the Levee Breaks."

The thing that separated these four Men from all the cock-rocking Boys was that they played with *feel*, with *funk*. As critic Ron Ross wrote in March 1975, "It's their unprecedented feel for rhythm and riff cranked up to nerve-numbing volume that makes Zeppelin perhaps the most successful rock and roll band of all time, and it's this awe-inspiring control of virtually violent sound that justifies that success."

Led Zeppelin was the greatest hard rock band of all not because they were pillaging, TV-trashing hedonists—they were and they weren't—but because they could *play*. Over the lean, sinewy bass lines of John Paul Jones and the deceptively straight stomping of John Bonham, you had the full-throttle-but-weirdly-girly yelp of Robert Plant and the crunching, multitextured guitar-shapes of Jimmy Page. Arguably, it was the most successful chemistry experiment ever conducted in the name of rock.

"I knew exactly the style I was after and the sort of musicians I wanted to play with, the sort of powerhouse sound I was really going for," Jimmy Page told Mick Houghton in 1976. "I guess it proves that the group was really meant to be, the way it all came together. And I was so lucky to find everybody so instantly, without making massive searches and doing numerous auditions that you hear about to fill the gaps."

From the word go—the double stab of the opening "Good Times, Bad Times," on the band's 1969 debut album—every recorded note and beat of Zeppelin's music simply careened out of the speakers. "That first album was the first time that headphones meant anything to me," Robert Plant recalled. "What I heard coming back to me over the cans while I was singing was better than the finest chick in all the land. It had so much weight, so much power, it was devastating."

"There just wasn't anything like it at that time," John Paul Jones reflected. "Jimmy's production was very innovative. And when Robert roared in, the initial reaction from people was, 'Where did you *find* him?'"

Of the many hard rock bands that came in Zeppelin's wake, few have come remotely close to the visceral, tight-but-loose grooves patented by Page, Plant, Jones, and Bonham. Some have made powerfully sensual metal—AC/DC on *Back in Black*, Metallica on *Metallica*, Queens of the Stone Age on *Songs for the Deaf*—but none has replicated the dark stew of

Led Zeppelin's sound. And that's without even mentioning the latter's beauteous acoustic flip side.

"Jimmy Page revolutionized everything," producer Rick Rubin told *Vanity Fair's* Lisa Robinson. "There was no real blues rock in that bombastic way before Zeppelin. Plus, with the insane drumming of John Bonham, it was radical, playing at a very, very high level—improvisational on a big-rock scale. It was brand new."

Of course, there was a time—the time of the punk wars—when Led Zeppelin's power had to be refuted, resisted, denied. By 1977, any music fan with an ounce of credibility felt obliged to dismiss Zeppelin as dinosaurs, to spit in the face of the stadium behemoth they had become. But once the punk dust had settled, we were all forced to return like contrite puppies, clinging once more to the great Zeppelin albums as life rafts through the desensitized and enervated '80s.

"The majority of the music was built on an extreme energy, obsessively extreme at times and joyously so," said Robert Plant. "Pagey's ability to take teeny-weeny bits and develop them into huge anthemic moments was stunning. And despite people's desire to think it was dark, it was just an enthusiasm to grab this music, and grab it so tight."

How ironic, then, when Led Zeppelin became the presiding animus of '90s guitar music, *the* platform for both grunge (Soundgarden, Smashing Pumpkins) and retro rock (the Cult, the Black Crowes). And how great, come the early years of the new century, to hear that spirit in every guitar lick and vocal snarl laid down by such blues-rooted bands as the White Stripes. Listen to "Little Bird" on the Stripes' brilliant *De Stijl* if you doubt me.

"'Little Bird' was definitely one of the moments where I thought, 'I *know* this sounds like Led Zeppelin, but I'm going to put it on the album anyway,'" Jack White said. "All my friends would come over and say, 'This is very Led Zeppelin.' And I'd say, 'I know it is.'"

"I love the way that Jack White says I was the thing he least liked about Led Zeppelin," said Robert Plant with a chuckle. "And I think, 'Well, that's fine, boy, but if you're going to play "In My Time of Dying," listen to the master.' But you know, that sound hasn't really been heard in the contemporary world, in bedsit-college land, since 1970. So its sudden re-emergence via the White Stripes is, like, 'Hey, what's *that*?'"

So what *was* it, exactly? In essence, a hybrid of volume and grace: of sex and spirit, metallic attack and poetic shimmer. A late-flowering bloom of Britain's '60s blues boom, Zeppelin was never a group of purists; they were musical mongrels from the start.

"It came together very quickly," said Jimmy Page. "Ultimately I wanted the group to be a marriage of blues, hard rock, and acoustic music with heavy choruses, a combination that hadn't been explored fully before: lots of light and shade in the music."

Talking to *NME*'s Chris Salewicz in 1977, Page expanded the point. Zeppelin's music, he said, possessed "the root [that] is in all rock and roll . . . the earthiness." But he added that it had "all the other facets that, shall we say, musicians of today have been able to get. You know, finger style, folk areas, and things like that. And traces of jazz. Generally the three strong areas. Which is so important."

Zeppelin's breathtaking eclecticism was immediately evident on their stunning debut album, released at the start of 1969. If its essential undertow was primordial blues ("You Shook Me," "I Can't Quit You, Baby"), its range was almost chameleonic, incorporating folk ("Babe, I'm Gonna Leave You"), Indian scales ("Black Mountain Side"), pop rock ("Your Time Is Gonna Come"), and even a sort of pro-to-punk rock ("Communication Breakdown"). "We like to play a cross section of styles," Page told *Melody Maker*'s Chris Welch early in 1970. "We're not a rabble-rousing group. We're trying to play some music."

If *Led Zeppelin II*, also released in 1969, was heavy on Heavy—with its storming übermetal masterpieces "Whole Lotta Love," "Heartbreaker," et al—the band still found room on the record for "Ramble On" and "Thank You," the first a Tolkien-imbued acoustic-into-electric beauty of a song, the second a plangent ode to Robert Plant's Indian-born wife, Maureen.

With *Led Zeppelin III* (1970), the group took their

biggest risk to date, packing the album with acoustic tracks that mystified the hard core of their fans. *III* blasted off with the fearsome "Immigrant Song," Zeppelin at their most mercilessly heavy, but offered pastoral alternatives in several of their finest ballads ("Tangerine," "That's the Way") and folk hollers ("Gallows Pole," "Bron-Y-Aur Stomp").

"The idea of using acoustic guitars and developing much more of a textural thing came about because, if we weren't careful, we were going to end up part of a whole Grand Funk Railroad/James Gang thing," Robert Plant said. "By the time 'Whole Lotta Love' had been such a *statement*, it was definitely time to veer over to the left and see how far we could take it in another direction."

The fourth Led Zeppelin album, the subject of this book, may be the most perfectly realized display of the group's range. Combining the electric density of *Led Zeppelin II* with the acoustic lacework of *Led Zeppelin III*, the album known variously as *Four Symbols*, *IV*, *"ZoSo,"* and ⚡🜚🜛🜜 offset the ferocious blues-rock grind of "Black Dog" with the golden utopianism of "Going to California," the chiming folk mandolins of "The Battle of Evermore" with the shuddering drive of "When the Levee Breaks," the nostalgic blast of "Rock and Roll" with the slow-building, multitiered "Stairway to Heaven."

"Music is very like a kaleidoscope," Robert Plant told *NME*'s Roy Carr in April 1972. "And I feel that particular album was just a case of us stretching out. It was a very natural development."

With 1975's double-album *Physical Graffiti*, Led Zeppelin arguably stretched out even more. But for all that "Kashmir" and "In My Time of Dying" remain towering peaks of the group's work, *Graffiti* has too many weak links, too many off-the-cuff sketches, to rival the fourth album—or even, in my estimation, the first three.

ZoSo⚒☻ⓘ stands like a monument in the landscape of rock and roll, a benchmark against which all rock albums are measured. Eight tracks long, it's a blueprint for the journey on which a great album should take you, from sludgy blues-metal to swampy demolition grooves via Little Richard drum intros, Fairport folk convention, medieval prog symphonics, and California dreaming. The fourth biggest-selling album of all time. It ranks behind the Eagles' Greatest Hits album. ZoSo⚒☻ⓘ also boasts in "Stairway to Heaven," the most-played track in American FM radio history.

ZoSo⚒☻ⓘ made Zeppelin's fans a global tribe of cultist devotees—suburban potheads turned disciples of darkness. With its runic symbols, its allusions to magic, and its gatefold-sleeve depiction of the Hermit of the Tarot, the album courted controversy from the moment of its release. Ever since, it has been a beacon for disaffected metalheads the world over. Jimmy Page's chosen symbol, misread as "ZoSo," became a diabolical touchstone for every small-town stoner in '70s America.

"By 1975, 'ZoSo' was painted or carved on every static thing rocker kids could find," wrote American sociologist Donna Gaines, PhD. "It had become a unifying symbol for America's suburban adolescents. The children of "ZoSo" are Zep's legacy. Mostly white males, nonaffluent American kids mixing up the old-school prole(tariat) values of their parents, mass culture, pagan yearnings, and '60s hedonism."

As much as the Rolling Stones defined the decadence of British rock bands for America, Zeppelin took the concept of satanic majesty a significant step further. Jimmy Page in particular, with his interest in the notorious occult writer Aleister Crowley, made the sinister foppishness of Mick Jagger and Keith Richards look tame. Stories of Page's and the band's touring antics—backstage and in hotel rooms—became part of rock folklore.

"Led Zeppelin . . . made records that fed this yen for power and enchantment, for hedonistic mystique," wrote Erik Davis in his brilliant 2005 study of ⚡️🜂⚗️⊙. The band, he noted, were "rock gods who staged their own *Götterdämmerung.*"

For the group itself, the stories ultimately detracted from the music. Notoriety overshadowed what was actually there in the grooves of their albums. "That whole lunacy thing was all people knew about us, and it was all word-of-mouth," Plant sighed to Cameron Crowe in 1975. "All those times of lunacy were okay, but we aren't and never were monsters. Just good-time boys, loved by their fans and hated by their critics."

⚡️🜂⚗️⊙

Thirty years later, Led Zeppelin's frontman maintained an uneasy relationship with his past. "No matter what you do," he told Sylvie Simmons in 2005, "there are people who are still waiting for the return of the four horsemen of the apocalypse. You only have to have a tiny, weeny bit of common sense to see that that's been and gone, the times are different now. . . ."

"There's no point in competing with my past," Plant told me in September 2003. "I mean, I'd love to work with Jimmy and John Paul, but I don't see how we could give it anything constructive without falling back into the sort of general melee of everybody's expectations."

Five months earlier, I'd met with Plant in Birmingham, the city in and around which he'd grown up. Freshly exposed to Led Zeppelin's might in the form of *DVD* and the 1973 live recording released as *How the West Was Won*, his pride was only too clear.

"It was such an amazing time, and things moved at such a rate of knots," he said. "And even though the currency of Led Zeppelin has been re-evaluated so many times for different reasons—out in the cold, back in again, big riffs, here comes the Cult—it's stunning stuff.

"Eighty percent of the time, Led Zeppelin was an absolute extravaganza. It was the greatest adventure of my life."

1

I'VE ONLY BEEN THIS YOUNG ONCE

THINGS WEREN'T looking up for young Robert Plant as he alighted at Pangbourne Station on a sultry afternoon in the summer of 1968. The Black Country boy with the big bluesy voice had sung with several promising bands and had even released a couple of singles, but he couldn't get a break and was beginning to despair of his career ever taking off. Traveling from Birmingham to Berkshire on that late July day, "it was the real desperation scene, man, like I had nowhere else to go."

Plant's old band, an outfit known as the Band of Joy, had played covers of songs by such West Coast bands as Love, Moby Grape, and Buffalo Springfield, in contrast to the blues and blue-eyed soul in which he had specialized just a couple of years earlier. Smitten with tales of free love and flower power in San

Francisco and Southern California, Robert had been reborn as a midlands hippie, a groovy androgyne with curly blond locks who dressed in loon pants and Carnaby Street caftans.

"I really just wanted to get to San Francisco and join up," Plant recalls. "I had so much empathy with the commentary in America at the time of Vietnam that I just wanted to be with Jack Casady and with Janis Joplin. There was some kind of fable being created there, and a social change that was taking place, and the music was a catalyst in all of that."

But if the Band of Joy's renditions of Buffalo Springfield songs had, in Plant's words, "saved me from ending up being the typical English pub singer," the group hadn't exactly set the world on fire. "There were very few other groups around at the time doing that sort of thing," Plant told the underground paper *International Times* the following spring. "Eventually we were getting sixty, seventy-five quid [or approximately $113–$142 US] a night. In the end, however, I just had to give it up. I thought, 'Bollocks [Crap], nobody wants to know.'" Later he claimed that "everyone in Birmingham was desperate to get out and join a successful band . . . everyone wanted to move to London."

As he stepped on to the platform at Pangbourne, a sedate town in the Thames Estuary, Plant's appearance caused a few eyebrows to rise: Carnaby Street this wasn't. Barely had the singer closed the door of the compartment behind him when he was set upon by an indignant matron of advancing years, berating him for his unkempt locks and effeminate apparel.

"There I was with my suitcase, and suddenly this old woman starts slapping my face and shouting about my hair," Plant told *International Times*. "Well, I was staggered, so I called a cop and he says it was my own fault for having long hair. So much for British justice."

Recovering from the assault, Plant found a taxi and asked the driver to convey him to a nearby boathouse on the river. He had come to see a guitarist whose hair was no shorter than his own, and who—just a few days before—had driven up to the midlands to watch Plant perform with his new group, the oddly named Hobstweedle.

Unlike Robert Plant, Jimmy Page's career was unmistakably on the rise. From the early '60s onward, "Little" Jimmy was one of the premier studio guitarists on the London music scene, adding his licks to literally hundreds of hits by artists as diverse as the Who, Lulu, and Val Doonican. He'd played on sessions for American producers Bert Berns and Burt Bacharach. He was seldom out of work.

There was another string to Page's bow, moreover: He could produce. Hours upon hours in London's recording studios had afforded him the opportunity to study the technical side of record production and to pick up tips from hitmakers such as Mickie Most (producer of the Animals, Herman's Hermits, and Donovan) and Shel Talmy (producer of the Kinks, the

Who, and Manfred Mann). By 1965, Page was sufficiently versed in recording techniques for Rolling Stones manager Andrew Loog Oldham to hire him as in-house producer for the new Immediate label.

The sunless, often subterranean world of studios wasn't enough for Page, however. He was tiring of the long hours and factory-line work of pop sessions. "Believe me, a lot of guys would consider that to be the apex—studio work," Page would say a decade later. "I was doing three studio dates a day, and I was becoming one of those sort of people that I hated."

Early in 1966, Page was approached by the Yardbirds, the R&B group that had provided a launching pad for the career of guitar deity Eric Clapton. Now featuring the equally dazzling guitarist Jeff Beck, the Yardbirds needed a replacement for bassist Paul Samwell-Smith. Page, all too aware of the drastic drop in income it would entail, stepped into the breach. It wasn't long before he was playing guitar rather than bass alongside Beck.

For an all-too-brief period in the fall of 1966, the two men played and recorded together in the Yardbirds as sparring partners, their intertwined licks heard on the far-out single "Happenings Ten Years Time Ago." But the band was never going to be big enough for both of them. "Tensions were rising within the group," recalls then-manager Simon Napier-Bell. "For Jimmy, the problem was that [the] solos were not his own creation. For Jeff, the problem was that Jimmy was stealing half his applause."

When the temperamental Beck quit the Yardbirds in October, Page found himself the lead guitarist in a group veering somewhat unsteadily from blues to pop and back.

If commercially the Yardbirds were in decline, Page's new prominence within the group gave him an opportunity not only to experiment as a guitarist but to tour the new psychedelic ballrooms of North America. At San Francisco's legendary acid palace, the Fillmore, gimmicks such as playing his guitar with a violin bow proved irresistible to the heads of Haight-Ashbury.

"On 'Glimpses' I was doing the bowed guitar thing, and I had tapes panning across the stage on this high-fidelity stereo sampler," Page says. "It was quite avant-garde stuff for the time."

With one foot in the 3-minute, 45-rpm pop era and the other in the new album-oriented world of rock, the Yardbirds were in danger of being left behind by hard-hitting new acts such as the Jimi Hendrix Experience; Eric Clapton's band, Cream; and even the new Jeff Beck Group. "The Yardbirds were quite powerful within their own right," Page recalled, "but Mickie Most was really just interested in singles and we were interested in albums."

There was one person who believed in the Yardbirds, however, and that was the man-mountain who'd taken over from Simon Napier-Bell as their manager. More accurately, Peter Grant believed in Jimmy Page, whose charisma was obvious from the minute he joined the band. Cool and beautiful in an almost effeminate way, Page looked like a new kind of pop star.

Napier-Bell had informed Grant that Page was a troublemaker, but Grant respected Page's financial acumen and resolved to fight for the band in their relationship with their record company. Years later, Grant's wife, Gloria, half-joked that her husband loved Jimmy more than he loved her.

"When I started managing the Yardbirds," Grant recalled, "they were not getting the hit singles but were on the college circuit and underground scene in America. Instead of trying to get played on Top 40 radio, I realized there was another market. We were the first UK act to get booked at places like the Fillmore. The scene was changing."

Grant, whose massive 6-foot-3-inch frame belied his early years as a wrestler, had worked in partnership with Mickie Most before striking out on his own as a manager. An intimidating if avuncular figure who'd toured with such rock-and-roll legends as Chuck Berry and Jerry Lee Lewis, Peter was astute enough to see that a new cult of the guitar hero was blossoming around Clapton, Hendrix, and Beck and that Page could be groomed as the next great gunslinger.

In the spring of 1968, the Yardbirds agreed to call it a day, with a final tour of the United States to complete. One afternoon before departing in March, Page and Grant drove around London's West End discussing what the future held. "We were in a traffic jam," Grant recalled, "and I said to Jimmy, 'What are you going to do? Do you want to go back to sessions or what?'" When Jimmy said he had some ideas for a new group and that he wanted to produce as well as play guitar, Grant said simply, "Let's do it."

The tour wound up in Montgomery, Alabama, in early June of 1968, with Page returning to London on June 15. After honoring a last UK commitment in Luton, the Yardbirds were no more. Uncertain of the right direction in which to go, Page and Peter Grant settled on the concept of "the New Yardbirds," looking to recruit new members alongside original bassist Chris Dreja.

The latter's first choice as a replacement for Relf, Mickie Most protégé Terry Reid, declined the job offer but pointed Page in the direction of a singer he described as "the Wild Man from the Black Country." Thirteen days after the Yardbirds' muted last hurrah, Page and Grant drove up to a teacher-training college in Birmingham to watch Robert Plant holler away in Hobstweedle. The band wasn't to Page's taste, but Plant's voice, presence, and sexuality were exactly what he was looking for.

"Robert was all right," Page said. "He was singing really well, although it was stuff that I didn't personally like very much. He was a Moby Grape fanatic, and the group was doing all of those semiobscure West Coast songs." Jimmy told John Tobler and

Stuart Grundy that "it seemed really strange . . . that somebody that good hadn't emerged before, but it always seems that at the end of the day, someone who's good will come through." He added that it "unnerved" him just to listen to Plant's "primeval wail," which had evolved from a Stevie Winwood pastiche to a goosebump-inducing shriek.

Page's first impression of Plant was of "a big, rug-headed kern [yokel]." Good-natured and curious, the Black Country boy was woefully unsophisticated compared to Page. Plant, by the same token, was overawed by the guitarist. "You can smell when people have traveled and had their doors opened a little wider than most," he said. "You could feel that was the deal with Jimmy."

Within minutes, the two young men were combing through Page's vinyl collection, pulling out albums and bonding over shared favorites by an eclectic assortment of artists. "We found we had exactly the same tastes in music," Plant said a few months later. LPs by Larry Williams, Don and Dewey, Incredible String Band, and Buddy Guy spilled across the floor. They played Muddy Waters' "You Shook Me" and Joan Baez's "Babe, I'm Gonna Leave You."

"I had a whole sort of repertoire in my mind of songs that I wanted to put into this new format," Page claimed in 2005. "[Songs] like 'Babe, I'm Gonna Leave You.' But it was all going to grow; I was seeing this dynamic. It wasn't down to one particular thing. It wasn't just the blues or rock and roll or folk music."

What struck Plant straightaway was the intensity of Page's musical drive—an almost feverish need to realize his musical vision. "I don't think I'd ever come across a personality like it before," the singer recalled. "He had a demeanor which you had to adjust to; certainly it wasn't very casual to start with."

Unlike Robert, who'd grown up in the bosom of an extended family and social circle, Jimmy was a born loner, an only child whose immersion in the guitar compensated for his lack of companionship.

"I was trying to build a band," Page says. "I knew what way it was going to go. I knew how to put the things in place, and I had a good idea of what style of vocalist I was looking for. The whole personality aspect does come into it, but initially the whole thing is, if you've got a bond musically and everyone's got that mutual respect for each other, it should work . . . at least for a little while."

Page, as it happened, had already been contacted by a bass guitarist—an outstanding musician who, like Page, was tiring of the day-in-day-out grind of London studio work. John Baldwin, who'd changed his name to the more fanciful "John Paul Jones," spotted a small news item in the music press announcing Page's intention to form his own band from the ashes of the Yardbirds. On July 19, he telephoned the guitarist to offer his services.

Page and Jones knew each other and had worked together on several occasions. "I'd heard of Pagey before I heard of Clapton or Beck," Jones has said of the former studio wunderkind. In addition to sessions they'd played together, Jones had arranged strings on the Yardbirds' 1967 single "Little Games."

By early August 1968, Chris Dreja was out of the "New Yardbirds" picture and Jones had clinched the bass spot in the group. "I jumped at the chance to get him," Page said. "Musically he's the best musician of us all. He had a proper training and he has quite brilliant ideas."

Jones, whose only experience of playing in a proper gigging band had been with ex-Shadows Jet Harris and Tony Meehan 5 years before, relished the chance to become part of a self-contained rock group. Wry and self-effacing, his personality offered a further contrast to the Page/Plant dynamic. "Jonesy," commented Plant, "was a bit . . . not *withdrawn*, but he stands back a little and shoots the odd little bit of dialogue into the air."

The final piece of Page's jigsaw—the drummer—proved the hardest to slot into place. This time the favored candidate came via Robert Plant. John "Bonzo" Bonham had known the singer for years as a fellow product of the music scene around Birmingham and the midlands. Indeed, he had played in the Band of Joy. "[Robert] knows me off by heart and vice versa," Bonzo told an early interviewer. "I think that's why we get on so well."

"Jimmy rang me up and says, 'I saw a drummer

last night and this guy plays so good and so loud, we must get him,'" Peter Grant recalled. But Bonham, already rated as one of the best drummers in England, was less convinced than John Paul Jones of the new group's long-term potential. Furthermore, he was earning a decent crust as a drummer-for-hire and had a wife and 2-year-old son to support. That summer found him playing behind American singer-songwriter Tim Rose.

"When I was asked to join the Yardbirds, I thought they'd been forgotten in England," Bonham explained later. "[But] I knew Jimmy was a highly respected guitarist, and Robert I'd known for years. So even if it didn't take off, it was a chance to play in a really good group."

On July 31, Jimmy Page and Peter Grant went to see Bonham play with Tim Rose at the Country Club in Hampstead. They instantly recognized that the power of John's drumming would be a priceless addition to the new band. In the first week of August, Bonham drove down to Pangbourne to meet Page. After a few more days of hesitation—and a flurry of pleading telegrams from Grant—he committed to the group.

On August 19, Jimmy Page's "New Yardbirds" convened for their first rehearsal in London's Chinatown. "We all met in this little room just to see if we could even stand each other," John Paul Jones remembered. "It was wall-to-wall amplifiers and terrible, all old. Robert had heard I was a sessionman, and he was wondering what was going to turn up—some old bloke with a pipe?"

"I don't think Jonesy's ever worked with anybody like me before," Plant remarked afterward. "Me not knowing any of the rudiments of music or anything like that, and not really desiring to learn them, but still hitting it off."

From the second they started bashing out "Train Kept a-Rollin'," an old Johnny Burnette Trio rocker that regularly featured in the Yardbirds' repertoire, the quartet felt like kismet. "Jimmy counted it out and the room just exploded," Jones recalled. "And we said, 'Right, we're on, this is it, this is going to work!' And we just sort of built it up from there."

"I've never been so turned on in my life," declared Robert Plant. "Although we were all steeped in blues and R&B, we found out in the first hour and a half that we had our own identity." Talking to Joe Smith in the late '80s, the singer admitted the sound wasn't pretty. "It wasn't *supposed* to be a pretty thing," he said. "It was just an unleashing of energy. But it felt like it was something I always wanted."

Within weeks, the group had pieced together a set list out of old Yardbirds numbers and blues covers. Howlin' Wolf's "How Many More Years" morphed into "How Many More Times." "Dazed and Confused," a song Page had discovered on an obscure album by American singer-songwriter Jake Holmes, became an extended epic and a vehicle for neopsychedelic jamming. "'Dazed and Confused' came from the Yardbirds," Page recalled. "That was my showcase, show-off bit with the bow." Playing "Dazed" onstage, Page turned into a satanic Paganini, an evil minstrel with his face obscured behind a curtain of black hair.

"Bonzo and I were already in the freakout zone after the Band of Joy, so it was quite natural for us to go into long solos and pauses and crescendos," Robert Plant says. "I mean, I listen to things like "How Many More Times" and it swings, and it's got all those '60s bits and pieces that could have come off a *Nuggets* album. For Jimmy, it was an extension of what he did, and for us, it was an extension of what *we* did."

A 2-week Yardbirds tour of Scandinavia having been booked by Peter Grant back in the summer, the radically remolded group made their live debut at the Gladsaxe Teen Club in Copenhagen on September 7, 1968—exactly 2 months to the day since the Yardbirds had played their swansong set in Luton.

"It was a tentative start," according to Robert Plant. "We didn't have half the recklessness that became, for me, the whole joy of Led Zeppelin." So powerful was Plant's voice, however, that when the speakers broke down at the band's first Stockholm show on September 12, in Page's words, "you could still hear his voice at the back of the auditorium over the entire group."

The band was still known as "the New Yardbirds" when they began 2 weeks of recording at Olympic

Studios in Barnes, southwest London, on September 27. With the sessions paid for upfront from Jimmy Page's savings, work proceeded apace. In all, the band logged little more than 30 hours at Olympic.

The album remains one of the great debuts in rock history, a magnificent showcase of the group's strengths. "Everything," said Robert Plant, "was fitting together into a trademark for us." The sound of Plant's voice alone—like Janis Joplin with testosterone—was formidable.

The opening track, "Good Times, Bad Times," immediately announced that we were in the presence of power—a new kind of energy pointing forward to the '70s, to bigger riffs and meatier beats. Bonham's drumming on the track was astounding, almost funky. "The most stunning thing about it, of course, is Bonzo's amazing kick drum," Jimmy Page said. "It's superhuman when you realize he was not playing with double kick. That's one kick drum! That's when people started understanding what he was all about."

To flow out of "Good Times, Bad Times" into the mournful folk drama of Anne Briggs's "Babe, I'm Gonna Leave You" was equally remarkable. The pathos and pain of Plant's vocal over Page's plangent picking, followed by thunderous strumming and drum rolls, was hair-raising.

"The music was so intense that *everything* was intense," Plant recalled of the sessions. "The ambition was intense and the delivery was intense. We all knew that this power was ridiculous from the beginning . . . so it was very hard to relax, sit down and have a beer and be the guys from the Black Country."

The band's "heavy" side was there in abundance in the viscous blues sludge of "You Shook Me" and the swampy bad-trip dread of "Dazed and Confused," both riding on the restrained power of the band's rhythm section.

"I immediately recognized Bonham's musicality," says John Paul Jones. "He kept a really straight groove on slow numbers, mainly because he could. And there aren't many that can—*really*. To play slow and groove is one of the hardest things in the world. So it was a joy to just sit back on a beat like 'You Shook Me' and just ride it."

Inspired by Eric Clapton—and before him by such Chicago masters as Otis Rush, Hubert Sumlin, Elmore James, and Buddy Guy—Page turned the Gibson Les Paul guitar into a cauterizing weapon. The Les Paul, Page told *Guitar World*'s Steven Rosen, had "a beautiful sustain to it, and I like sustain because it relates to bowed instruments and everything; this whole area that everyone's been pushing and experimenting in. When you think about it, it's mainly sustain."

But it wasn't just fat sustain tones that Page specialized in. On that first album, he created radically different sounds for virtually every track. "When people talk about how good other guitarists are,"

Robert Plant told Nigel Williamson, "they're talking about how they play within the accepted structures of contemporary guitar playing, while Jimmy plays miles outside of it."

In "Black Mountain Side," there was a second outing for Page's acoustic guitar on the album. An homage of sorts to his folk-guitar idol Bert Jansch (and specifically, the latter's classic "Black Waterside"), the track was a companion piece to "White Summer," an instrumental adaptation of the folk traditional "She Moves Through the Fair," which appeared on the Yardbirds' *Little Games* album. Both pieces were in D-A-D-G-A-D tuning and featured the Indian hand drums known as tabla.

The album's remaining tracks rounded the set out brilliantly: a reverential reading of Otis Rush's "I Can't Quit You, Baby," a Stooges-esque proto-punk classic in "Communication Breakdown," the loping, brutish "How Many More Times," and the choral, organ-graced "Your Time Is Gonna Come." "We were a completely untried group of people," Jimmy Page told Ritchie Yorke, "who got together to [make an album] that really had only one ingredient that we were sure of—genuine enthusiasm."

If the material had a grab-bag feel, the production was awesomely dense. This was the new sound of hard rock, trampling everything underfoot and leaving '60s pop for dead.

"Having worked in the studios for so long as a session player," Page later recalled, "I had been in so many sessions where the drummer was stuck in a little booth and he would be hitting the drums for all he was worth and it would just sound as though he was hitting a cardboard box. I knew that drums would have to breathe to have that proper sound, to have that ambience. So consequently, we were working on the ambience of everything, of the instruments, all the way through."

With the album completed, the group played their first UK dates, still billed as the Yardbirds. The name, however, was on its last legs. "We realized we were working under false pretences," Page admitted. "The thing had quickly gone beyond where the Yardbirds had left off. We all agreed that there was no point in retaining the Yardbirds tag, so . . . we decided to change the name. It was a fresh beginning for us all."

Playing its last date with the old name at Liverpool University on Saturday, October 19, the band a week later finally became Led Zeppelin, a moniker inspired by a throwaway line of Keith Moon's. "Moon had made a joke about going down like a lead Zeppelin," Peter Grant recalled. "In the circumstances, the name seemed perfect. I got rid of the A. I was doodling in the office and it just looked better, and I also didn't want any confusion over the pronunciation in America."

The first Led Zeppelin gig took place at Bristol's Boxing Club on Saturday, October 26, 1968. It was hardly an auspicious start. "It was a tryout for their big hype launch," remembered Russell Hunter of support act, the Deviants. "The audience hated us and despised them. When [they] came on, they got through a number and a half until the fire extinguishers, buckets, bricks, and everything was being thrown at them."

Things were very different when Zeppelin played London's Marquee on December 10. "I went out early afternoon from our office on Oxford Street to Wardour Street," Peter Grant remembered. "And I thought, 'Fuck me, what's this queue?' There were about 200 already lined up. That's when I knew that we just wouldn't need the media. It was going to be about the fans."

But Grant's real goal was North America, where big bucks were to be made. "Peter had his eyes set on something I couldn't even imagine," said Robert Plant.

In November, Grant flew to New York to discuss a deal with Atlantic Records. Jerry Wexler, the company's vice president, secretly despised loud guitar rock but wanted to match his partner Ahmet Ertegun's earlier signing of Cream, who wrapped their farewell tour in Rhode Island on November 2. Aware of Jimmy Page from Bert Berns's mid-'60s Atlantic sessions in London, Wexler had been further encouraged by the endorsement of his latest UK signing, Dusty Springfield (for whom John Paul Jones had arranged a session in late August, after he'd already agreed to join Page's band).

Columbia's Clive Davis and Reprise's Mo Ostin were also in the race to sign Led Zeppelin, but Wexler, in his own words, "prevailed by offering a 5-year contract with a £75,000 [or appoximately $143,000 US] advance for the first year and four 1-year options." In the end, Atlantic stumped up £110,000 [or approximately $210,000 US]. "I was proud of the signing," Wexler wrote in his autobiography, "but as it turned out, I didn't really hang out with the group. Ahmet [Ertegun] got along famously with them (and Peter Grant)."

For 1968, the Zeppelin deal was unheard-of, testament to Atlantic's confidence in both Page and Grant and in what they heard on the Olympic tapes. "In one of the biggest deals of the year," Bob Rolontz wrote in the company's press release, "Atlantic Records has signed the hot new English group, Led Zeppelin, to a long-term, exclusive recording contract. Although the exact terms of the deal are secret, it can be disclosed that it is one of the most substantial deals Atlantic has ever made."

From the band's point of view, to be the first white rock group on such a legendary label—sometime home to Ray Charles and Aretha Franklin—was a major honor. "As far as I know, we were the first white band on Atlantic, because all the earlier white bands had been on Atco," says Page. "At the time, we said we'd really like to be on Atlantic as opposed to Atco, because it was the first true independent label that had really sailed through and done it well."

The deal done, it was time for Led Zeppelin to take their music across the ocean. America was calling.

2

REALLY GOT TO RAMBLE

PETER GRANT'S instincts about America were quickly proved right. Led Zeppelin seemed to be made for a country where young white males, in particular, craved louder, heavier sounds. "I can't really comment on just why we broke so big in the States," Jimmy Page told *NME*'s Nick Kent. "I can only think that we were aware of dynamics at a time when everyone was into that drawn-out West Coast style of playing."

For Robert Plant and John Bonham, arriving in Los Angeles just before Christmas, America was a mind-skewering culture shock. Chauffered to the Chateau Marmont on Sunset Boulevard by tour manager Richard Cole, Zeppelin was quickly plunged into the fun and frolics of the LA rock scene. A gallery of freaks and groupies from the stable of Frank Zappa's Straight and Bizarre labels was ensconced at the Marmont and swiftly took the English quartet to their collective bosom.

"We ended up in the suite Burl Ives had just vacated," Plant recalled of the hotel. "Down the corridor were the GTOs [Girls Together Outrageously], Wild Man Fischer, and all those Sunset Strip characters of the time. Rodney Binghenheimer was making coffee . . . [and] all that dour Englishness swiftly disappeared into the powder-blue, post–Summer of Love Californian sunshine. I was teleported."

For Plant, America was a vast garden of unlimited opportunities. "I was 22 and I was going, 'Fucking hell, I *want* some of that,'" he says. "'And then I want some of *that*, and then can you get me some Charley Patton? And who's that girl over there and what's in that packet?' There was no perception of taste, no decorum."

Booked by heavyweight promoter Frank Barsalona as the support act on a tour headlined by Atlantic act Vanilla Fudge, Led Zeppelin was virtually an unknown quantity in America. "We came over here and nobody knew who we were, and we weren't following anything," Plant said in 1971. "We weren't saying, 'It's Gary Puckett for us, and come over here.'"

"Jimmy was an old hand at America," said Richard Cole. "But the others were all relatively new to working there, and I think they had to feel the audience out and get comfortable with it. Vanilla Fudge was a big band, so Zeppelin wasn't playing to 50 people. I'm sure it was quite intimidating."

Almost instantly, however, the band made people

sit up and take notice. The standard of their musicianship alone was enough to blow Vanilla Fudge clean off the stage. "All of a sudden, the name of the band traveled like wildfire," said Jimmy Page. "We were supporting bands and they weren't turning up, because we were really quite an intimidating force."

"The biggest happening of the 1969 heavy rock scene is Led Zeppelin," *NME*'s US correspondent June Harris wrote after the band's debut album climbed into the American Top 10 in May. "The reaction to the group's first tour here has not only been incredible, it's been nothing short of sensational."

Key gigs on Zeppelin's first coast-to-coast sortie in early 1969 included shows at the Kinetic Playground in Chicago, Page's old haunt the Fillmore in San Francisco, and—on the East Coast—the Boston Tea Party. "As far as I'm concerned, the key gig . . . was one that we played [in Boston]," John Paul Jones told Nick Kent. "The audience just wouldn't let us off the stage. . . . When we finally left the stage, we'd played for 4-plus hours. Peter was absolutely ecstatic. He was crying, if you can imagine that, and hugging us all."

Anyone who really knew Peter Grant—or "G," as the band often referred to him—could have imagined his tears of pride and joy. "Peter lived, breathed, and slept beside the band," observed another, equally notorious manager named Malcolm McLaren. "[He] indulged in the same things they did."

"Jimmy said to me, 'The difference between Peter and other managers was Peter genuinely loved his bands,'" Richard Cole remembered. "Peter loved Maggie Bell, he loved Terry Reid, and he'd loved Rod [Stewart] and Jeff [Beck]. It wasn't just a money-making machine for him."

Significantly, Grant never had a written contract with Led Zeppelin. "We just had a gentlemen's agreement," John Paul Jones told Chris Welch. "He got the normal management fees and royalties from records as executive producer. [It was] all pretty above board, and as a result, it was a really happy band."

"Peter never let anybody near us," Jones said. "Record companies in those days had less say than they do now in what their artists do, but they had no say whatsoever in what we did."

If Jimmy Page had any misgivings about his group at this early stage, they were solely to do with Robert Plant's stage presence. "[He] did lack a bit of confidence at first, and I used to hide all the negative reviews we had," Peter Grant recalled. "But come mid-'69, he was well in the swing of it."

"I didn't even know what to do with my arms," Plant says. "Now I understand why Joe Cocker did that thing for a while, because what are you going to do? There were so many solos!"

As the tour progressed, Led Zeppelin became an ever more assured live act, shaking America's stages to their foundations. Onstage there seemed to be a kind of telepathy between the four men—one that enabled them to take songs in almost any direction they chose.

"Led Zeppelin's live performance was so important to the sum of the parts," Jimmy Page said. "We'd go onstage, and if all four of us were really on top of it, it would just take on this fifth dimension. Improvisation and spontaneity were happening all the time, and that was the beauty of it."

"Led Zeppelin was an extravaganza," said Robert Plant. "There were songs that began and ended cut-and-dried—"Communication Breakdown," "Good Times, Bad Times." But the thing about the group was the extension of the instrumental parts, and that was in full fling by the time we even made our first record. And now, if you look at all the sort of bits and pieces I used to throw in for my own enjoyment—I mean, it's a bit corny now, because it's referring to Eddie Cochran or Elvis—it was what we feasted on to get riffs, to get organized, to become a big band with big riffs."

Something that communicated itself from the earliest days of Led Zeppelin was the balance of power within the group. Although Page was the founder and putative leader of the group, he never hogged the limelight or lorded it over his comrades. He'd seen the damage Jeff Beck's ego had done to the Yardbirds and was determined to avoid that in Led Zeppelin. The tensions and skirmishes that blighted such Zeppelin prototypes as the Who were nowhere to be seen in this quasi-supergroup.

"The groups that did have a good sound were successful, but they always seemed to have internal troubles," John Paul Jones noted, "while the groups who did get on with each other never got heard. Somehow you had to get the two elements together—an amicable group and good sound—plus exposure."

"The only ones that used to row were Bonham and Plant," said Richard Cole. "But that had nothing to do with musical direction. It would be something that went on when the two of them were driving home to Birmingham or something. One of them wouldn't want to pay for the gas, things that were so amusing to the other four of us. They had history, they were very close, and they'd both come into the band as outsiders, so their arguments were like two brothers arguing. But it was never malicious."

"What you put out, you get back again all the time," Page told Nick Kent. "The band is a good example of that simply because there's an amazing chemistry at work there, if only astrologically. Astrologically it's very powerful indeed. Robert's the perfect frontman Leo . . . John Paul Jones and I are stoic Capricorns, Bonzo the Gemini."

"A lot of it came from Pagey," says former Zeppelin roadie Henry Smith, who'd worked with Page in the Yardbirds days. "He was very centered, very quiet. He knew himself. And I think that had a lot to do with the chemistry of the band, because those were the types of people that he sought out when he went to start his band. Jeff Beck was like the high-school bully, and Jimmy wasn't that way."

"There were really no camps in Led Zeppelin," said Jones. "People think it was, like, Jimmy and Robert were always together, so that left the rhythm section. But it was always the southerners and the midlanders. Jimmy and I would take the piss out of Robert and Bonzo, and they'd call us poncey [snobby] southern so-and-sos. But the four of us were very protective of Led Zeppelin."

The relationship between Page and Plant was itself complementary rather than competitive. Physical opposites, Page was as introverted and inscrutable as Plant was open and expansive. If there were echoes of Jagger and Richards in the duality of the erotic frontman and his shadowy foil, there was less of the Stones' indecent chumminess in Led Zeppelin. Page was the conductor of the group's sound, Plant his primary emotional vent. Unlike Jagger, too, Plant was modest and self-doubting, frequently prone to stage fright.

Interestingly, one gay Zeppelin fan described the two men as "a more dangerous and more androgynous 'version' of Mick and Keith," thereby setting up a compelling juxtaposition with the apparent machismo of their music. Certainly there was something soft and pretty about Plant, with his barmaid curls, blousey shirts, and camp stage movements, in the same way that there was something effeminate about the darker, more glamorous Page.

The band's machismo, as it happened, was already a cause of complaint by early 1969, with critics flinching at what they heard as the phallic bombast of Led Zeppelin's "heavy metal" sound. Zeppelin itself always took issue with its alleged paternity of metal. Both Page and Plant used the term *virility* in describing the group's music but resented the way HM was laid at their door. Lumped in with such crass, post-Cream "power trios" as Mountain and Grand Funk Railroad, Zeppelin was persistently misheard as purveyors of Neanderthal riffs for stoned headbangers.

When *The Rolling Stone History of Rock & Roll* later stated that "the basic formula for heavy metal was codified [by Led Zeppelin]: blues chords plus high-pitched male tenor vocals singing lyrics that ideally combined mysticism, sexism, and hostility," its authors were only half right. For a start, real heavy metal requires a strong element of the Gothic, which Zeppelin never had; second, the charge of "hostility" simply doesn't stand up when you inspect the band's lyrics. Most important, perhaps, Zeppelin's "heavy" rock was so much subtler, sexier, and more multitextured than anything a group like Black Sabbath ever produced.

"[Heavy metal] is a bastard term to us," Page complained. "I can't relate that to us because the thing that comes to mind when people say heavy metal is riff-bashing, and I don't think we ever just did riff-bashing at any point. It was always inner dynamics, light and shade, drama and versatility that we were going for."

American critics, perhaps resentful of the group's almost instant success, carped at Led Zeppelin in a chorus of disdain.

"Like their predecessors," *Rolling Stone*'s Jon Landau wrote in 1969, "they build their style on doubling bass and guitar figures, thereby creating a distorted emphasis on the bottom sound range. It is a completely physical approach to sound that usually works better live than on records. Zeppelin's demeanor was loud, impersonal, exhibitionistic, violent, and often insane. Watching them at a recent concert, I saw little more than Robert Plant's imitations of sexuality and Jimmy Page's unwillingness to sustain a musical idea for more than a few measures."

The feud between the band and the press became a paradoxical feature of Led Zeppelin's illustrious career, though it only cemented the solidarity between the four of them.

"Instead of just transposing what happens and saying it was accepted," Plant said despairingly in 1971, "[critics] suddenly start becoming an entity for themselves instead of a courier for the people. . . . If we get all these blasé attitudes at an early stage where we're still trying to prove to a lot of people that it's a wholesome, positive thing and they keep tearing away inside it, well, it'll be ruined before it's even gotten halfway."

Nor was it just critics who jeered. The band's own peers—no doubt threatened—turned on them with vaguely catty remarks. Pete Townshend poo-pooh'd "solo-guitar-based groups" that did better in America than in England. Eric Clapton thought Zeppelin was "unnecessarily loud." Keith Richards said Plant's voice "started to get on my nerves."

If the put-downs affected the band, it didn't show in the music they assembled for their second album. A tour de force of pulverizing riffs and febrile blues-ology, *Led Zeppelin II* stands at the gateway to the '70s as a monstrously powerful record. "Led Zeppelin [has] taken the best aspects of the Yardbirds' style and the British flash blues tradition," Lester Bangs wrote in *Creem*, "and inflated them into a mighty war machine."

Against all the odds, moreover, *Led Zeppelin II* was made on the hoof as the band continued their onslaught of the US concert circuit. "The first album had been created in a very crisp, businesslike fashion," Plant says. "*Zeppelin II*, on the other hand, was written and recorded mostly on the road."

"Album two was insane," Page told *Disc* in April 1972. "We'd put down a rhythm track in London, add the voice in New York, put in harmonica in Vancouver, then come back to New York to do the mixing."

ZoSo △⊕Ⓘ

Although the group got under way with the album at Olympic Studios in April 1969, laying down basic tracks for "Whole Lotta Love," "Ramble On," and "What Is and What Should Never Be," their departure for America that month necessitated sessions at A&R, Mirror Sound, and Juggy Sound in New York, and at other studios that could be accommodated by the punishing itinerary set up by Peter Grant.

More than anything, *Led Zeppelin II* is Jimmy Page's record—an incredible collection of what Robert Plant called "the mightiest riffs in the world." "Any tribute [that] flows in must go to Jimmy and his riffs," said John Paul Jones, who thought the bruising "Whole Lotta Love" had probably been born during one of the many "Dazed and Confused" jams. "They were mostly in the key of E, and you could really play around with them . . . the whole thing, the whole band really, came straight from the blues."

"When I was 5 years old," said Jack White of the White Stripes, "there was a tape at a girl's house in her basement and "Whole Lotta Love" was on it. And I had rewound it so many times that there was a fuck-up in the tape before the guitar solo. I still think that solo is some of the greatest guitar anyone's ever played, if not the greatest. Just that little section is so powerful, and it was powerful to me when I was 5 years old. And whenever it comes on the radio now, I still want to rewind that part."

Most of the riffs on *Zeppelin II* are blues-rooted—

brooding, squalling Les Paul chords overlaid by brighter, glossier licks. But this isn't the workaday post–John Mayall hippie blues of Savoy Brown, Chicken Shack, or early Fleetwood Mac; it's down-and-dirty, primeval sex music, blues with what John Bonham called thrutch. "It was still blues-based," Robert Plant told Nigel Williamson, "but it was a much more carnal approach to the music and quite flamboyant."

"The Lemon Song" adapted "Killing Floor" by Howlin' Wolf, most savage of all the bluesmen who migrated north to Chicago. "Whole Lotta Love" was itself a lift from Muddy Waters's "You Need Love," whose composer Willie Dixon later received an out-of-court settlement for the song. Dixon also later received money for the album's closing track "Bring It On Home," based on a Sonny Boy Williamson song of the same name.

Led Zeppelin's "reliance" on the blues has many detractors, of course. Like every rock band that emerged from the British blues boom of the '60s, Zeppelin pilfered riffs from African Americans who'd already been ripped off by their original contracts in the '40s and '50s.

It is certainly one of the less attractive aspects of Jimmy Page that he seemed so callously indifferent to the implications of this purloining, often taking song-writing credit where none was merited. Genius may steal where talent borrows, but Page—probably encouraged by Peter Grant, who himself had plenty to gain—was more brazen about it than most.

"I think when Willie Dixon turned on the radio in Chicago 20 years after he wrote his blues, he thought, 'That's my song,'" Robert Plant said in 1985. "When we ripped it off, I said to Jimmy, 'Hey, that's not our song.' And he said, 'Shut up and keep walking.'"

Page craftily threw this allegation back in Plant's face in an interview with *Guitar World*. "Robert was supposed to change the lyrics, and he didn't always do that," he said. "[That's] what brought on most of the grief. They couldn't get us on the guitar parts of the music, but they nailed us on the lyrics. So anyway, if there is any plagiarism, just blame Robert."

Blues isn't all we hear on *Led Zeppelin II*, of course. Plant himself weighed in with major contributions to "Ramble On" and "Thank You," the first a Tolkien-inspired beauty that switched brilliantly from acoustic strumming to electric dynamics, the second a heartfelt hymn to his wife, featuring John Paul Jones on organ.

"In the early days, I was writing the lyrics as well as the music, because Robert hadn't written before," Jimmy Page recalled. "It took a lot of ribbing and teasing to actually get him into writing, which was funny. And then on the second LP, he wrote the words of "Thank You"—he said, 'I'd like to have a crack at this and write it for my wife.'" Plant claimed that it had "taken a long time, a lot of insecurity and nerves and the 'I'm a failure' stuff" to produce the lyrics for the two songs.

"Moby Dick," meanwhile, showcased the might of John Bonham at a time when drum solos were becoming de rigueur at rock gigs. Bonzo's playing on *Led Zeppelin II* in general confirmed that he was an astounding drummer.

"I yell out when I'm playing," Bonham told *Disc* in June 1972. "I yell like a bear to give it a boost. I like it to be like a thunderstorm."

In contrast to the epicene foppishness of Page and Plant, there *was* something of the bear about Bonzo. Not a teddy bear, mind you, but more a ferocious and probably drunken grizzly. A Birmingham thug possessed of uncanny rhythmic coordination, Bonham was the absolute core of what made Led Zeppelin great.

"He was a great drummer, whether it was a heavy death march or an acoustic thing with small animals cavorting in the meadow," said Andy Johns, who would soon be engineering for the band. "[He was] a naturally fantastic timekeeper and not a trudge merchant, very creative with sound."

"[Bonzo] had a lot of input into the riffs we played, more than he was credited for, I'd say," John Paul Jones reflected. "He would change the whole flavor of a piece, and lots of our numbers would start out with a drum pattern. We'd build a riff around the drums."

"I'm not trying to be any superstar," Bonham told *Melody Maker*'s Roy Hollingworth in June 1972.

"I just do my bit as one-quarter of Led Zeppelin. When I have a solo, I don't ever imagine drummers around watching me. I don't try to impress people who play the drums. I play for people. I don't try to perform the most amazing changes in tempo . . . it would take away the essence of Jimmy's guitar and Robert's voice. John Paul and myself lay down a thick backdrop; that's what we do."

In front of a lesser, showier rhythm section, Page and Plant would never have shone so brightly. "You can feel it coming from behind," Plant told *Sounds*'s Steve Peacock in June 1971. "The bass and drums suddenly knit together, and it's like a big handshake between the two and they go off, and Jimmy and I'll stay doing something else. It's like a good jigsaw puzzle."

One of the biggest lies ever told about Led Zeppelin was that their music boiled down to volume and power. When Robert Christgau—"dean of American rock critics"—called Bonham "ham-handed," you had to wonder what he was listening to. Gene Krupa he may not have been; thoughtless, Bonzo never was. Every fill he played was a little work of art, simple but unique in feel.

"Because it doesn't swing, [Led Zeppelin's music] doesn't set the audience dancing," the English critic Mick Gold wrote. "It aims for the temples, not the feet, and its total effect is one of stupefaction."

Doesn't swing?! Listen to the funky propulsion of

"Whole Lotta Love," to the explosive breaks on "What Is and What Should Never Be," "Bring It On Home," and the splendidly lewd "The Lemon Song" and tell me Led Zeppelin doesn't swing. Thank God the American critic Robert Palmer, writing some years after Gold, noted that after years of crunching hip-hop drum loops, "[Zeppelin's] lurching beats and staggered rhythms sound a lot different: They swing like mad."

"You could dance to Led Zeppelin," says John Paul Jones, who'd been as influenced by Motown maestro James Jamerson as by Chess stalwart Willie Dixon. "Blues wasn't our only experience of black music. Bonzo and I were both into soul and R&B, and I was into jazz as well."

In addition to the riffs and "swing" of *Led Zeppelin II,* the album was a production triumph. If the band's debut had upped the ante for rock's new sonic power, *Led Zeppelin II* left '60s pop for dead. "The goal was synaesthesia," Page said. "Creating pictures with sound."

Critic Ron Ross related such "synaesthesia" to the growing use of "immobilizing" drugs such as marijuana and downers, especially used in conjunction with state-of-the-art headphones. "For many younger teens psychedelic exploration gave way to heavy metal surrender," Ross wrote. "Page's approach to producing Zeppelin's rhythm section seemed to be to create a cavernously resonant bottom with a rock-steady groove that the listener could lay back on like a mattress, while the stereo speakers threw Jimmy's scintillating solos at him from everywhere at once with piercing psychologically surgical precision."

"The whole secret of it," Page said, "is that all you need to do is something that's got a solid, substantial riff underneath it. We were still doing that but putting interesting, quirky melodies on top of it."

If Eric Clapton had been "God," Page's use of effects—panning, phasing, backward reverb, and the like—made him a sonic sorcerer. In some respects, too, this aural sorcery compensated for his occasional sloppiness, both live and in the studio.

"As a musician," Page told Steven Rosen with surprising candor, "I think my greatest achievement has been to create unexpected melodies and harmonies within a rock-and-roll framework. My guitar playing developed because I had that great unit to work with. I don't really have a technique, as such, when you think of people with technique. But I think it's harder to come up with fresh ideas, fresh approaches, and a fresh vision."

For Page, the real goal was to create sonic pictures that moved people, stirring emotion in the listener. His touchstones, significantly, were not '60s acts such as the Beatles or the Stones but the great blues and rockabilly artists of the preceding decade. He had, after all, learned guitar by playing along to Elvis Presley's "Baby, Let's Play House."

"I still feel that some so-called progressive groups have gone too far with their personalized intellectualization of beat music," Page told *Record Mirror* in February 1970. "I don't want our music complicated by that kind of ego trip—our music is essentially emotional like the old rock stars of the past. It's difficult to listen to those early Presley records and not feel something. We are not going out to make any kind of moral or political statement. Our music is simply us."

Harking back to the Sun Records era didn't alter the fact that, in the words of Donna Gaines, "Led Zeppelin's grubby, velvet-ruffled sex-bombast slammed us right into the '70s." The toppling of the Beatles' *Abbey Road* from the No. 1 spot on America's album chart by *Led Zeppelin II* was symbolic of the new order that Page, Plant, Jones, and Bonham ushered in.

Equally symbolic was Led Zeppelin's anger at Atlantic's decision to release "Whole Lotta Love" as a single. The band decided that from then on, it would have no dealings with vinyl at 45 rpm. The '70s, for them, would be about albums as self-contained wholes, suites of songs rather than ephemeral radio fodder.

"I always thought of the Stones as a pop group who made singles," Plant said, looking back to the time. "What we said was there's no point in putting out a single when the album is the statement of the band. It sounds quite pompous now, but underneath it all, that was quite true."

As if bearing out Plant's convictions, Zeppelin's second album stayed on the American charts for months, sustained by the band's constant touring. Between December 26, 1968, and April 18, 1970, the group played no less than 153 shows, their nightly fee rapidly escalating from $500 to a basic guarantee of $100,000. Peter Grant's patient strategy had paid off.

"We didn't go to Madison Square Garden straight off," Grant recalled. "It was gradually built up in all those states like North Carolina. It's like we built it up into an event. In fact, that was when I came up with that 'An Evening with Led Zeppelin' tag. I know it was corny, but it was like the old '30s stage line. I guess that was a by-product of my days as a 14-year-old stage hand."

Nothing in the band's life would ever be the same again. "Playing music is a very sexual act," Jimmy Page told *Disc* in April 1972. "But once you earn money, people start assuming things about you and your whole life is changed. You get involved in high finance."

3

A SOMEWHAT FORGOTTEN PICTURE OF TRUE COMPLETENESS

AT THE DAWN of the '70s, Led Zeppelin was in pole position. They'd bludgeoned America into submission, stepping into the breach that opened up when Eric Clapton slowed his hand, Jimi Hendrix freed the gypsy funkateer within, and everyone else went solo.

"To begin with, we arrived on the scene at just the right time in America as Cream had disbanded and Hendrix was into other things," Jimmy Page told *Record Mirror* in February 1970. "I think our initial success was due to the fact that so many of the good American groups were moving toward softer sounds, which made our heavy rock approach more dramatic."

Yet the spark had failed to ignite in the band's own homeland, not least because the British press refused to buy what they perceived as hype. "I think our success in America had an effect on the critique over [here]," said Robert Plant. "It was like, 'They've gone, and who the fuck are they anyway? Oh well, it's overblown . . .'"

To rectify this, Peter Grant—who hadn't helped matters by giving his production company the ironic name Superhype Music, Inc.—set up a short UK tour for the New Year. Kicking off in Bristol and taking in the Plant/Bonham parish of Birmingham, the tour hit London's venerable Royal Albert Hall on January 9.

"We did some touring in England," said John Paul Jones, "but it was much harder to get anywhere here because the press wasn't very interested. So maybe the Albert Hall was the first sort of 'here we are' type of show in England. I've heard it reported that some of the press thought we were an American band."

What is fantastic about the Albert Hall footage on *DVD* is how stark and elemental it is. There are no trippy lights here, no dry-ice clouds or Jaggeresque preening. Just four men, barely more than boys, bound together in intense rhythmic symbiosis, rooted in the most brutal, pulverizing grooves ever devised: "Dazed and Confused," "Whole Lotta Love," "Communication Breakdown," "How Many More Times."

John Paul Jones—a heavy metal monk. John Bonham—all moustache and muscles. Jimmy Page in a sleeveless harlequin sweater. Robert Plant's pre-

Raphaelite face all but obscured behind a flaming mane of hair.

"At the Albert Hall, I was 21, and I was just a Black Country hippie," the singer says. "I was hanging on for dear life, weaving my way through the three greatest players of their time. It was an absolute shock when I first saw that footage. It's so disarming—not unnerving but kind of cute and coy, and you see all that sort of naivety and the absolute *wonder* of what we were doing. And the *freshness* of it, because the whole sort of stereotypical rock-singer thing hadn't kicked in for me."

"The power came from the music," says John Paul Jones. "You didn't notice that there wasn't a set, because the music drew you in. And there wasn't much leaping about the stage, because everybody was working hard and concentrating. People say to me, 'You can just see the communication on the stage, and my band doesn't do that. It's like we're all in separate bands.' Our priority in Led Zeppelin was to make Led Zeppelin sound great, and if that meant playing two notes in a bar and shutting up for a bit, that's what it took."

At the end of March 1970, Zeppelin took its empathy and telepathy back to America. It was their fifth US tour in 18 months, and this time it was less of a blast. With the country in the throes of Vietnam-related violence—the Kent State campus shootings were just around the corner—the band was on edge.

Peter Grant and road manager Richard Cole got into scrapes with promoters. John Bonham became homesick and restless, taking out his feelings on hotel rooms. A show had to be stopped when a brawl erupted in Pittsburgh. Another promoter pulled a gun on Grant in Memphis. Southern cops hassled the limey longhairs. Plant suffered stage fright. "More than anyone," wrote Richard Cole, "Robert seemed on the brink of collapse."

"I don't think we can take America again for a while," John Paul Jones remarked on their return. "America definitely unhinges you. The knack is to hinge yourself up again when you get back."

"We'd toured on the strength of the first album," says Jimmy Page, "and then we just toured and toured and toured. In between times, we fitted in a small amount of recording at Olympic, where we did part of "Ramble On" and "Whole Lotta Love" and a couple of others, and the rest of *Led Zeppelin II* was recorded at various times, and finally I mixed it with Eddie Kramer in New York. And then we were touring on the strength of the *second* album. And finally we had a real break, and it was probably only a couple of months, but to us it seemed an eternity."

Back in England in the last week of April, Jones and Bonham scuttled back to the safety of their new rock-star homes. Jones had moved into a big house in Chorleywood, Hertfordshire, with his wife, Mo, and their two daughters. Bonham had swapped the caravan he'd shared with his wife, Pat, for a farmhouse and 15 acres at West Hagley, outside Birmingham.

But there was no extended rest for the wicked, or at least for the band's principal songwriters. Apart from any other considerations, Atlantic was owed another album. For a change of scenery, and perhaps inspiration, Plant suggested to Page that they hole up with partners—plus Plant's baby daughter, Carmen, and dog, Strider—in a remote Welsh cottage called Bron-Yr-Aur (pronounced "Bron-raar"). It was a place Plant had often visited in his boyhood.

"Jimmy and I are going to rent a little cottage near the River Dyfi in Wales," Robert told *Disc* in March 1970. "[It's a place] where we can lock ourselves away for a few weeks just to see what we can come up with when there's no one else around."

"Robert had this place that he'd been to with his parents in the past, and he asked if I fancied coming down there," recalls Page. "I said it would do me a lot of good to get out to the countryside. And what came out on our third album was a reflection of the fact that the pendulum had swung in the total opposite direction from all that *Led Zeppelin II* live thing and the energy of being on the road. It was like, 'Oh, we're here, we're in nature, we can hear the birds sing, there's not a car sound, there's no airplanes, there's no concert to do.' It was just fantastic."

So fantastic that Page and his French girlfriend, Charlotte Martin, conceived their daughter, Scarlet, at Bron-Yr-Aur, not long after he and Plant had been on the long walk that led to the writing of "That's the Way," just one of several folkish songs to be included on *Led Zeppelin III*. The cottage—Page and Plant's version of the Band's Big Pink—may also have inspired Page to purchase his own bucolic retreat on the shores of Loch Ness. Boleskine House was the former residence of Satanist magus Aleister Crowley, about whom the guitarist was rather enthusiastic.

"It was time to step back, take stock, and not get lost in it all," Plant told Cameron Crowe. "Zeppelin was starting to get very big, and we wanted the rest of our journey to take a level course. Hence the trip into the mountains and the beginning of the ethereal Page and Plant. I thought we'd be able to get a little peace and quiet and get your actual Californian, Marin County blues."

Accompanying the party were Zeppelin roadies Clive Coulson and Sandy McGregor, there to help with more domestic issues such as groceries, transportation, and firewood. "Me and Sandy were the cooks, bottlewashers, and general slaves," Coulson recalled. "Pagey was the tea man. Plant's specialty was posing and telling people how to do things." Water came from a nearby stream and was heated on hot plates for washing. Baths had to be taken at the Owen Glendower hotel in nearby Machynlleth.

Folk had already been heard, of course, on Led Zeppelin's debut: in "Babe, I'm Gonna Leave You," in

"Black Mountain Side." Shortly before departing for Bron-Yr-Aur, Page performed "Black Mountain Side" together with "White Summer" on Julie Felix's TV Show *Once More with Felix*. He'd also included the two numbers in Zeppelin's set at San Francisco's Fillmore West on January 10, 1969. But for the two men, there was now a need to give proper space to this side of Zeppelin.

"I'm obsessed—not just interested, obsessed—with folk music," Page told *Sounds*'s Jonh [sic] Ingham in 1976. "[With] street music, the parallels between a country's street music and its so-called classical and intellectual music, the way certain scales have traveled right across the globe. All this ethnological and musical interaction fascinates me."

One afternoon, Page and Plant went for a walk, an acoustic guitar strapped to the former's back and a small tape recorder in his pocket. "We stopped and sat down," remembered Page. "I played the tune and Robert sang a verse straight off." *"I don't know how I'm gonna tell you,"* Plant sang, *"I can't play with you no more...."* The gorgeous "That's the Way" (aka "The Boy Next Door") arrived almost fully formed in that inspired moment, the sun just setting over a ravine, the hedgerows bustling. The experience brought the two men closer together. "Living together at Bron-Yr-Aur," Page told Zeppelin biographer Ritchie Yorke, "was the first time I really came to know Robert."

In Wales, Page and Plant sketched out the songs that made up the bulk of Led Zeppelin's acoustic repertoire for years to come. In addition to "That's the Way," they included the rollicking "Bron-Y-Aur Stomp" [sic], the traditional "Gallows Pole," the Tyrannosaurus-Rex–esque "Friends," plus "Hey Hey, What Can I Do" (B-side of "Immigrant Song"), "Over the Hills and Far Away" (*Houses of the Holy*), "Down by the Seaside," "The Rover," "Bron-Yr-Aur" (*Physical Graffiti*), and "Poor Tom" (*Coda*), the latter again very reminiscent of Marc Bolan in his cosmic-folkie days. (On a bootleg version of "Bron-Y-Aur Stomp" one can hear the gleeful giggling of a child who must be Carmen Plant.)

Originally entitled "Jennings Farm Blues," after the farm near Kidderminster that Plant had recently bought for £8,000 (or approximately $15,238 US), "Bron-Y-Aur Stomp" perfectly captured the bucolic merriment Page and Plant experienced at the cottage. The stomp in question was a kind of love song to Strider: "*Walk down the country lanes, I'll be singin' a song, I'll be callin' your name/Hear the wind whisper in the trees that Mother Nature's proud of you and me.*"

"We wrote those songs and walked and talked and thought and went off to the Abbey where they hid the Grail," Plant recalls. "No matter how cute and comical it might be now to look back at that, it gave us so much energy, because we were really *close* to something. We *believed*. It was absolutely wonderful, and my heart was so light and happy. At that time, at that age, 1970 was like the biggest blue sky I ever saw."

When Page and Plant returned to London with "That's the Way," "Friends," and "Bron-Y-Aur Stomp," Jones and Bonham quickly took the new material in their stride. "Jimmy had always had acoustic guitars lying around," Jones said. "It was very organic. Suddenly we found ourselves with a bit more time, and we sat down with some acoustic instruments, and we started exploring."

Jones had himself acquired a mandolin that he'd purchased on tour in America. "I'd probably learned my first mandolin tunes from Fairport Convention's *Liege and Lief*," he remembered. "I mean, there was more folk-rock about, and there were people like Poco and Matthews Southern Comfort, and like any curious musician you just start playing it."

"The evocation of the 'folk-' or acoustic-based music in Led Zeppelin," Susan Fast wrote in *Houses of the Holy*, ". . . helps shape the band's mythology in terms of linking them to ideals of (perceived) non-commercialism, simplicity, the feeling of intimacy that came with such musical means. . . ."

The ramshackle, "noncommercial" spirit of Bron-Yr-Aur carried through to sessions at Headley Grange, a damp Hampshire mansion to which the band decamped in mid-May. "Rather than waste a lot of studio time thinking of the riffs and lyrics in the studio,"

John Paul Jones told *Disc* in November 1970, "we decided this place in Hampshire was definitely the best place to get the numbers down before we went there."

"Headley Grange was found by our secretary, Carole Browne," said Richard Cole. "She used to read those magazines like *The Lady*, and she'd read that this place was for rent. I think she sent a dispatch rider down there to see if it was suitable and had enough rooms and if they could put a mobile studio in there. It wasn't very comfortable. I mean, the band was used to five-star hotels and had lovely homes by now."

"Apparently, it was a Victorian workhouse at one time," said Jimmy Page, who'd spent summers as a boy at his great-uncle's manor house in Northamptonshire. "It was a pretty austere place; I loved the atmosphere of it. I really did, personally. The others got a bit spooked out by it."

"Jimmy thought he'd seen a ghost there too," said Andy Johns, the engineer brought in for the sessions. "The rest of us moaned about being cold, but Jimmy was more concerned with creepy noises or flying fucking furniture."

Said Richard Cole, "I sometimes think they recorded in the worst places imaginable because, in the back of Jimmy's mind, it meant they had to get on with it so they could get out of there." (When Zeppelin returned to Headley Grange on a third visit in 1974—this time with a mobile unit belonging to Ronnie Lane of the Faces—Cole booked them into a swanky hotel called the Frencham Ponds. "Page stayed behind at Headley," laughs Cole. "He was quite happy in that fuckin' horrible cold house.")

Headley Grange had been built in 1795 as a "House of Industry" to shelter infirm or aged paupers, along with orphans and illegitimate children. It's hard to believe it was a happy place. On November 23, 1830, a mob of rioters sacked the house, after which it was repaired and continued to be used as a workhouse. It was sold in 1870 to a builder for £420 (or approximately $800 US) and converted into a private house renamed Headley Grange.

A private residence for almost a hundred years, in the 1960s it became a temporary home for visiting Americans, then a hostel for students from the nearby Farnham School of Art. By the end of that decade, it was being regularly used as a rehearsal and recording facility by such bands as Fleetwood Mac and the Pretty Things. "It was magic for me because I knew the area pretty well," Peter Grant remembers. "I'd been evacuated there in the war."

"Maybe the spark of actually being in Bron-Yr-Aur came into fruition when we said, 'Let's go to Headley Grange,'" Jimmy Page reflected. "I knew other bands had been there to rehearse, like Fleetwood Mac. It was like, 'Let's go to Headley with a mobile truck, and let's see what comes out of it all.'" The truck in question belonged to the Rolling Stones.

"At Headley, it was literally sitting around a fire

and picking things up and trying them out," said John Paul Jones. "There was no conscious desire along the lines of, 'Oh, we've done Heavy, now we should look at Soft,' and thank goodness." Jones also savored the pleasures of "sitting out on the grass a lot playing acoustic guitars and mandolins."

Plant later made the point that acoustic guitars did not per se signify gentler emotion. "It might be acoustic instrumentation," he told *Record Mirror* in March 1972, "but it's the venom or the bite or the drive, or it's the life or it's just what comes from behind. Things like "Friends" could never be done electrically with so much balls."

There was in any case a generous helping of Heavy on *Led Zeppelin III*: "Celebration Day" and "Out on the Tiles" were classic Zeppelin pile drivers, and the closing "Hats Off to (Roy) Harper" was a crazed slide-guitar shredding of Bukka White's "Shake 'em On Down." A trip to Iceland in the early summer fueled the writing of the mighty "Immigrant Song," a thunderous Viking threnody delivered in Plant's most cod-heroic wail. "'Immigrant Song' was supposed to be powerful *and* funny," Plant said. "People go, 'Zeppelin had a sense of *humor*?'"

On the sleeve of *Led Zeppelin III*, released in October 1970, credit was given to the "small derelict cottage in South Snowdonia" for "painting a somewhat forgotten picture of true completeness, which acted as an incentive to some of these musical statements."

For Plant, the album was a coming-of-age, as well as being the by-product of the band's growing links with such folk avatars as Roy Harper, Fairport Convention, and the Incredible String Band.

"The places that the String Band were coming from were places that we loved very much," the singer said. "But because I was a blues shouter and Pagey was out of the Yardbirds, we didn't have that pastoral kick. So hanging out with the String Band was pretty great. It was part bluff and part absolute ecstasy, and the Zeppelin thing was moving into that area in its own way, going from 'You Shook Me' to 'That's the Way.' *Zeppelin III* was something we felt good about because it would have been more obvious to use 'Whole Lotta Love' as a kind of calling card and carry on in that direction."

"I'm not sure that they didn't change direction and do the acoustic thing on *Led Zeppelin III*, knowing that they were going to go back to the other side," ventured Richard Cole. "The third album was almost like a break in the pattern. They didn't want to make it look like that was all they could do. Then when the fourth one came out, there was no dispute as to what they were about."

On June 28, with Robert Plant sporting a pointy dishevelled beard and Jimmy Page attired like a rock-and-roll farmer in floppy hat and tweed overcoat, the band played to 150,000 people at the Bath Festival of Blues and Progressive Music, alongside of a slew of

Plant's Californian heroes—the Mothers, the Byrds, Santana, Country Joe and the Fish, Jefferson Airplane. This was the legendary occasion when Peter Grant pulled the plug on hapless electric-violin act the Flock in order for his boys to take the stage to the backdrop of a glorious sunset.

"As soon as Zeppelin ripped into their first number, the living field of people exploded," *Disc* reported. Along with set staples such as "Dazed and Confused," the band played the new "Since I've Been Loving You" and "That's the Way," still at that point known as "The Boy Next Door." The vibe at Bath was benign, a long way from the violence the band had experienced on recent American dates.

"I'd like to say a couple of things," Plant announced from the stage. "We've been playing in America a lot recently and we really thought, coming back here, we might have a dodgy time. There's a lot of things going wrong in America at the moment. Things are getting a bit sticky and whatnot. It's really nice to come to an open-air festival where there's no bad things happening."

Zeppelin's appearance at the festival made exactly the difference Grant had hoped for. Fans appreciated the sacrifice the group had made in turning down far more lucrative appearances in America. Subsequently, Zeppelin was regarded in Britain as the equals of the Stones and the Who.

July found the band in Notting Hill Gate, hunkered

down at Island Studios on Basing Street. The tortured blues ballad "Since I've Been Loving You" would be another of *Led Zeppelin III*'s electric highlights. It remains one of Plant's greatest vocal performances—Janis Joplin reborn as a lovelorn Black Country bricklayer.

"I can see Robert at the mike now," recalled Richard Digby-Smith, the young tape-op on the session. "He was so passionate. Lived every line. What you got on the record is what happened. His only preparation was an herbal cigarette and a couple of shots of Jack Daniel's."

"I don't know where it came from," said Plant of the song, "but the musical progression at the end of each verse—the chord choice—is not a natural place to go. And it's that *lift* up there that's so regal and so emotional. I don't know whether that was born from the loins of Jimmy or John Paul, but I know that when we reached that point in the song you could get a lump in the throat from being in the middle of it."

Led Zeppelin III was finally wrapped while Zeppelin was in the midst of its sixth US tour, which commenced in Cincinnati on August 5. (Page flew to Memphis to complete mixing at Ardent Studios later in the month. Ardent engineer Terry Manning said that when he was there, Jimmy overdubbed "the best rock guitar solo of all time" on "Since I've Been Loving You.") With *Led Zeppelin II* still high in the US charts, the group capitalized still further on their burgeoning reputation. For two nights in September, a new breed of headbangers packed Madison Square Garden for two September nights, coughing up a cool $200,000 for the privilege. Critics nonetheless continued to sneer.

The reaction to *Led Zeppelin III*, released in early October 1970, said it all: Having proved it was about so much more than power, the band was now pilloried precisely for going acoustic. Some reviewers implied that Zeppelin was merely imitating Crosby, Stills, Nash, Young and friends. "They missed the point altogether," Page told *NME*'s Chris Salewicz in 1977. "They forgot that we'd used acoustic guitars very heavily on the first album." Not that the reviews affected the album's skyrocketing sales for a minute: In its second week, it topped the US album chart and stayed there for a month. (Even so, *Led Zeppelin III* has long been the weakest-selling of the group's first four albums.)

"It didn't really start bothering me until after the third album," Page later told *Guitar World*. "After all we had accomplished, the press was still calling us a hype."

"If we were crap and they said we were crap, well, fair enough," said John Paul Jones. "But we were really good and we couldn't understand what the agenda was. We felt they'd missed the point. And the problem was that we then put up a defensive shield. Unfortunately, if defensive shields are successful, they defend against the good stuff as well as the bad stuff."

"When we talk about that time," Robert Plant reflected, "we have to understand that the press itself was a completely different animal: beer-swilling, monosyllabic guys who reviewed gigs from the beer tent. I don't think Nick Kent had surfaced, and Lester Bangs and those guys in America, the real poets, weren't involved in what we're talking about here. We weren't even visible, and yet we were everywhere. And that gave it even more power."

Bangs, who himself wrote of Led Zeppelin's "insensitive grossness," admitted that he "kept nursing this love-hate attitude" toward the group. Reviewing *Led Zeppelin III* for *Rolling Stone*, he noted that "That's the Way" was "the first song they've ever done that's truly moved me."

Whatever the critics felt, the band regarded *Led Zeppelin III* as a vital stepping-stone in their development. "I've talked to you before," Plant told *Melody Maker*'s Chris Welch in September 1970, "and probably given you the impression that I believed Zeppelin was never going to do what I wanted to do. But the new album is really getting there." He later claimed that, "It wasn't until *Led Zeppelin III* that I was able to calm it down and have the confidence to sing in a different style."

For Plant, the third album "showed there was a bit

more attached to us . . . than that "Shake Your Money-Maker" sort of stuff." The "simple thunder" of tracks such as "Heartbreaker" was, he said, "easier to assimilate" but "you can't just do that, otherwise you become stagnant and you're not really doing anything, you're just pleasing everybody else."

A quarter-century later, observing that "the cottage album" had been "incredibly important for my dignity," Plant went so far as to describe *Led Zeppelin III* as "our single most important achievement."

4

FLAMES FROM THE DRAGON OF DARKNESS

BY THE END of September 1970, Led Zeppelin had toured America six times. Exhausted by the constant air travel, the band craved another break. "We were fed up with going to America," Jimmy Page told *NME*'s Charles Shaar Murray in June 1973. "We'd been going twice a year, and at that time, America was really a trial, an effort."

Back in England, the group repeated what they had done in the spring. Jones and Bonham slunk off home while Page and Plant hightailed it to Bron-Yr-Aur in late October. "What we wanted to do was to continue with the momentum of the thread, which was ever onward," says Page.

"It was just four of us this time," says Henry Smith, the roadie who accompanied Page and Plant to the cottage with Sandy McGregor. "Jimmy, Robert, Sandy, and myself. No wives, no Peter, no Richard, no nobody else. I think we were there for about a week."

Among the things Page worked on that week was a sketch for an epic new song that would provide the centerpiece for the fourth album—and maybe supplant "Dazed and Confused" as the *pièce de résistance* of Zeppelin's live repertoire.

"It just felt like a good thing," said Henry Smith. "Like, if you want to write, you need to get away, and this was a great place to go to get away because there was *nobody* around. It was *so* off the beaten path. We were in the middle of a sheep field as I remember, and the sheep would almost come into the house while Jimmy and Robert were working on songs."

For Smith, it quickly became clear that Plant was far more of a country boy than Page. "I remember there was a little stream that was nearby," Henry said. "Robert and I were laying in the grass by the stream, parting the grass and looking at all the creatures and things running around in there. Robert was working on a song and used some of that feel of what we were doing for the song."

By the time the band was back at Island Studios in December, winding down this most profitable of years, the introduction to "Stairway to Heaven" was complete. As others have pointed out, the intro's descending chords sound remarkably like the Spirit instrumental "Taurus," though the resolution in the final bar is different. (It's likely that Page would have heard the track, given that Plant was an avid fan of the LA band. Indeed, he'd been to see Spirit play at Mother's in Birmingham early in 1970, suffering a car accident on the way home to Kidderminster.)

Work also began on the track that became "Four Sticks." The studio vibe, however, wasn't right; once again, Zeppelin felt the urge to decamp—to "get it together in the country," in the rock parlance of the times.

"It's better to do it all the way we do now, because you haven't got so many distractions," John Paul Jones told *Disc*. "We've done a good deal: [we've] broken the back of it, and recording starts this month. But rather than waste a lot of studio time thinking of the riffs and lyrics in the studio, we decided this place in Hampshire was definitely the best place to get the numbers down before we were there."

"You really do need the sort of facilities where you can take a break for a cup of tea and a wander [around] the garden, and then go back in and do whatever you have to do," Jimmy Page told Zeppelin biographer Ritchie Yorke. "Instead of that feeling of walking into a studio, down a flight of steps and into fluorescent lights . . . and opening up the big soundproof door and being surrounded by acoustic tiles. To work like that . . . you've got to program yourself. You're walking down those stairs telling yourself that you're going to play the solo of your life. But you so rarely do in those conditions. It's that hospital atmosphere that all studios have."

Initially, the band considered the rather more comfortable option of renting Mick Jagger's country house, Stargroves—also in Hampshire—for the sessions. Jimmy Page, however, turned out to be as penny-pinching as Jagger himself.

"Jimmy had the nickname 'Led Wallet,' and it's true that he was a bit tight," recalled Andy Johns, who'd recently done some engineering on the Rolling Stones's *Sticky Fingers* album at Stargroves and was now on board for Zeppelin's fourth album. "Mick Jagger had offered us his baronial mansion for £1,000 [or approximately $1,906 US] a week and Jimmy wouldn't pay it." Come the New Year, it was back to Headley Grange.

Plant and Bonham arrived together in one of the latter's many cars. Page, who'd never learned to drive, was driven down to Hampshire by Richard Cole. "I taught Jimmy to drive, but he never took his test," Cole says. "He had an Austin Champ Jeep we used to drive into Berkshire."

Jones, as was his wont, pitched up last. Headley in the winter was even more unprepossessing than it had been the previous spring. "[It] was horrible," Jones complained. "It was cold and damp . . . virtually no furniture, no pool table, no pub nearby. . . ." Jones recalled that they all "ran in when we arrived in a mad scramble to get the driest rooms." But once their roadies had got the fireplaces going—and Page had laid claim to a room on the third floor that came with a small electric fire—the band quickly settled in.

"It's that old cliché about a place in the country, but it was really great," Plant told Canadian journalist Rick McGrath. "The mikes coming in through the windows and a fire going in the hearth and people coming in with cups of tea and cakes and people tripping over leads, and the whole thing is utter chaos . . . it was a good feeling, and we did it as easy as pie."

Richard Cole says Zeppelin ate like "million-dollar Boy Scouts" at Headley Grange, lubricated by copious quantities of alcohol. Wearing a gamekeeper's cap and tweed jacket, Bonham frequently withdrew to the nearest pub after the band had knocked off for the day.

"There weren't any serious drugs around the band at that point," Cole added. "Just dope and a bit of coke. We had an account at a shop in the village, and we'd go down there regularly and collect huge quantities of cider. They were playing at being country squires. They found an old shotgun and used to shoot at squirrels in the woods, not that they ever hit any. And there was this lovely old black Labrador wandering around [that] we used to feed."

To the outside world—or at any rate the media—it seemed that Led Zeppelin had gone into hiding. As if to compensate for the lack of information, the music weeklies ran speculative news stories about rumors

ZoSo △◉ ①

that the group was splitting—unfounded tattle that Peter Grant declined to dignify with a response.

The band spent a week writing, arranging, and rehearsing before the Rolling Stones's mobile truck arrived at Headley. "We were keeping pretty regular hours together," Jimmy Page recalled, "even though they may not have been regular hours for most people."

A number of songs—at varying stages of composition—were given run-throughs. But there were many other half-finished (and in some cases half-recorded) contenders for inclusion on an album—enough, in fact, for the band to consider making the LP a double, or more eccentrically releasing four separate EPs.

"No Quarter," stemming from a keyboard piece by John Paul Jones, would appear in more brooding form on *Houses of the Holy*; "Boogie with Stu," like the antinuclear "Night Flight" and the Neil Young–esque "Down by the Seaside," would show up on *Physical Graffiti*. "The Rover," also included on *Graffiti*, was a song that then existed only in rudimentary acoustic form. Talking to Bob Harris on *The Old Grey Whistle Test* in 1975, Plant referred to this and other material on *Graffiti* as "old, crazy stuff . . . really good stuff that we thought, 'We can't keep it in the can any longer. . . .'"

Other songs fleetingly attempted at Headley Grange included "I Wanna Be Her Man," another nod of sorts to Neil Young, and a version of blues legend Leroy Carr's "Sloppy Drunk" featuring Page on mandolin and Plant himself on primitive guitar. "Robert wrote the lyrics again for this album," Page said, "but now he's getting more into playing the guitar himself, and he also plays drums; he finds that bits of melodies and riffs are also coming to him. Robert still hasn't plucked up the courage to play guitar on stage, but he is progressing well . . ." ("Sloppy Drunk," however, may simply have been a working title for "The Battle of Evermore"—and a reference to the duo's intoxicated mood.) *Houses of the Holy*'s "Dancing Days" may also have been given a run-through at Headley.

As with the first three, the fourth Zeppelin album began with a rapid assessment of the available material. "It was very spontaneous most of the time in Led Zeppelin," Plant told Joe Smith. "Things were created virtually as a four-piece band. It was Jimmy Page bringing in cassettes or ideas that were then created on the spot. Sometimes John Paul Jones would contribute the main leading part of a song, and then it would be a pretty quick arrangement of bits and pieces so that the thing fitted together rather quickly."

"Whenever we got together from the third, fourth, fifth album," Page told Stuart Grundy and John Tobler, ". . . we would always say 'What have you got?' to anybody else, to see if Jonesy had anything, to be honest. Robert and I were doing all the writing up to that point, unless it was a number . . . like a blues number. For instance, "When the Levee Breaks" is, and then we would make a split between the four of us. We were always trying to encourage [Jones] to come up with bits and pieces, so to speak, because that's usually what they were; he never came up with a complete whole song or anything."

One of the "bits and pieces" Jones brought to Headley Grange was a complex blues riff suggested to him by Muddy Waters's "psychedelic blues" album *Electric Mud*. "One track is a long rambling riff," Jones told Dave Lewis, "and I really liked the idea of writing something like that—a riff that would be like a linear journey. The idea came on a train coming back from Page's Pangbourne house. From the first run-through at the Grange, we knew it was a good one."

Actually, the first run-through of "Black Dog"— so known because of the Labrador who wandered about Headley Grange and its grounds—was a shambles that had all four men in stitches. "It was originally all in 3/16 time," said Jones, "but no one could keep up with that." The rhythmic changes that Jones, Page, and Bonham devised for the track were so intricate—Page called the song "a bit of a hairy one"—they were almost impossible to play. Particularly confounding was the B section after the first verse, a passage (commencing 41 seconds into the released take) in which Page's riff is completely out of synch with Bonham's 4/4 drum pattern.

"We were messing around when the other lads

suddenly came up with that passage on 'Black Dog,'" Plant told Ritchie Yorke. "They just played it, fell about all over the floor for 10 minutes in fits of laughter, played it again, burst into more laughter, then put it down on tape."

"When I wrote it," Jones told Susan Fast, "the B section of the riff was actually phrased as three 9/8 bars and one 5/8 bar over the straight 4/4, but nobody else could play it!" Jones maintains that they solved the conundrum of this "turnaround" section simply by counting four-time through as if there *were* no turnaround.

"I told Bonzo he had to keep playing four-to-the-bar all the way through," Jones added, ". . . but in the turnaround there is a 5/8 rhythm over the top. If you go through enough 5/8s, it arrives back on the beat." Jones stated that he wanted the riff "to turn back on itself."

To these ears, after all these years, the turnaround of "Black Dog" still sounds rhythmically wrong. In the words of Keith Shadwick, "no matter how many times you hear it, your ears are torn in two. . . ." A bootleg of the band working out the riffs at Headley Grange shows Bonham initially trying to stay more in step with Page's guitar rather than ploughing his own furrow through the song. Instead the band made a conscious decision to go for the impossible.

"You can't play it," Plant admitted in 1983. "Because it's got a beat that's a count of five over a count of four, and trips and skips and stuff like that. It was our prerogative and our joy to take what people thought. . . . We just wanted to see people try to move to it and then miss the beat. And then still call it heavy. It was just a trick, a game, and well within our capabilities to do. And it just stopped a lot of other people from doing the same thing, from copying it." (It almost stopped Led Zeppelin too: At a show later that year in Rochester, New York, "Black Dog" completely fell apart and would have ground to a complete halt had Page not winged his way out of the chaos with a blaringly loud solo.)

Even without the jarring turnaround section, "Black Dog" is one of the most fiendishly intricate songs in all of rock and roll. John Reid of the Hampton String Quartet, which performs an instrumental version of the song, claims the song "has something like 98 time-signature changes." It is also one of the most diabolically powerful tracks in the Led Zeppelin catalog—in the words of Guns N' Roses guitarist Slash, "the biggest, baddest, sexiest riff out there."

But which riff does Slash mean? There are so many interlinked in one continuous, unfurling sequence in the song, with the only real "breaks" or punctuations being Plant's a capella vocal phrases, starting with the immortal and unforgettable *"Hey hey, mama, said the way you move. . . ."* Inspired by Fleetwood Mac's "Oh Well," these hollered interpolations turn out to have been Page's idea.

"[Jonesy] had this great riff . . . and I added some sections to it as well and then we had the ideas," Jimmy told Stuart Grundy and John Tobler. "Actually, I must be totally honest, I suggested how you get the breaks with the vocals. That's it, I've finally owned up, as no one else will in the band. But that was the idea, to give it the vocal thing and then bring the riffs in."

Amusingly, if you listen carefully to "Black Dog," you can hear Bonzo clicking his sticks behind Plant before the band comes in, for example, on 12 seconds, 23 seconds, 35 seconds. "He did that to keep time and to signal the band," Page said. "We tried to eliminate most of them, but muting was much more difficult in those days than it is now."

The song itself has inspired much debate and conjecture over the years. For those obsessed with Page's diabolism, the title was assumed to refer to some hound of hell. For such listeners, the line *"eyes that shine, burnin' red"* seems to carry satanic resonance, or at least to suggest that the woman driving Plant mad is some evil harpy.

True, the lyric juxtaposes the girl with a *"steady-rollin' woman"* who won't tell him no lies or spend his money while *"tellin' her friends she gonna be a star."* (Is this fiendish temptress really just a groupie gold-digger?) But Erik Davis is surely right when he concludes that the burning eyes belong to Plant himself and that the song demonizes not "woman's sexual power" but "the male's own lust, experienced as a possession from within." Moreover the implication is that, unable to *"get my fill,"* Percy returns powerlessly to the honey-dripping "pretty baby" in the song's last verse.

Plant himself didn't read too much into "Black Dog." "I put a lot of work into my lyrics," he told Cameron Crowe. "Not all my stuff is meant to be scrutinized, though. Things like 'Black Dog' are blatant let's-do-it-in-the-bath-type things, but they make their point just the same."

"Black Dog" was in more or less finished form when the Rolling Stones's mobile unit—complete with accompanying technician Ian "Stu" Stewart, aka "the sixth Stone"—arrived in late January. Parking the truck around the back of the house, Andy Johns ran microphone leads through the windows of the drawing room, whose walls were covered with empty egg cartons that served as acoustic baffles. "Andy was a joy to work with," said Henry Smith. "He was such a nice guy, it was like he was your brother."

"[The truck] is a bit narrow, like a corridor, so your ability to monitor a situation isn't as good as in a proper studio," Johns recalled. "You end up talking to the band through a closed-circuit camera and a microphone instead of through the studio glass. It can get a bit impersonal, but the advantage is that the band is more at home. At a place like . . . Headley Grange, you had a fireplace, people bringing you cups of tea. It's much nicer than a studio."

"It seemed ideal," Page said. "As soon as we thought of an idea, we put it down on tape. In a way, it was a good method. The only thing wrong was that we'd get so excited about an idea that we'd really rush to finish its format, to get it on tape. It was like a quick productivity thing. It was just so exciting to have all the facilities there." Page's priority at this stage was to capture "a really good bass and drum sound," since he knew he could polish his guitar parts in overdubs after basic tracking.

For Robert Plant, the Headley Grange sessions evolved "bit by bit" into "a great collage" of tracks. "A studio is an immediate imposition," he told *Disc*'s Caroline Boucher in February, shortly over the sessions were over. "It's quite a limiting thing compared to sitting around a fire playing away, and we've been able to experiment with drum sounds by using just one microphone and things. At times it sounds like early Presley records drumming." Talking to *Sounds*'s Steve Peacock in June, Plant said the mood at Headley Grange was "bang!" "We could hear the results immediately," he said. "There was no big scene about going back into the studio and doing it again. . . ."

One of the first experiments the band attempted was setting up John Bonham's kit outside the drawing room, at the foot of Headley Grange's staircase (known as "the Minstrel Gallery"). "It was a sort of three-story house with a huge open hall and a staircase going up," Page told Stuart Grundy and John

Tobler. "That's where we got the classic drum sound on 'When the Levee Breaks.' We had the drums in the hall and sometimes the drums were in the room as well, and the amplifiers were all over. When Bonzo was in the hall, Jones and I were out there with earphones, the two sets of amps were in the other rooms and other parts such as cupboards and things. A very odd way of recording, but it certainly worked."

"We used to try everything," said John Paul Jones. "Basically, if you're a guitar-bass-drums band, you've got to come up with something a bit different each time so all the tracks don't sound the same. We used to have amps everywhere—in rooms, up stairwells, in bathrooms, outside the building. One of the advantages of not working in a studio was that in an old house you could always find an old cupboard to stick a guitar amp in."

"We hire this recording truck and trudge off to some cruddy old house in the country," Plant reminisced in 1974. "The last thing you'd expect is the music to fall right into place. But it does. We even spent one night sitting around drinking ourselves under the table, telling each other how good we were."

The mobile-truck setup at Headley Grange encouraged a spontaneity that hadn't been present even for the *Led Zeppelin III* sessions the previous year. Working, for example, on "Four Sticks," the song's loose-rolling riff was proving hard to harness. Intended as a trance-like raga with Indian overtones—Page and Plant re-recorded it the following year with a group of musicians in Bombay—it had the band flummoxed and frustrated. Page recalled attempting the song "on numerous occasions" without success.

Exasperation led to inspiration, however. Fed up with "Four Sticks," John Bonham emptied a can of Double Diamond lager down his throat and bashed out Earl Palmer's intro to Little Richard's 1957 hit "Keep-a-Knockin.'" Suddenly, the tension in the room dissipated as Page weighed in with an up-tempo riff from the Chuck Berry manual of vintage rock and roll.

"I played the riff automatically," Page recalled, "[and] we got through the whole of the 12-bar bit. We said, 'This is great, forget 'Four Sticks,' let's work on this.'" It was, he said, "a spontaneous combustion number." He later claimed the song was written in 15 minutes and recorded in three takes, complete with an Ian Stewart piano contribution that was worthy of Chuck Berry's immortal 88-key sideman Johnnie Johnson. (Stewart also featured on the self-explanatory "Boogie with Stu," a throwaway jam based on Richie Valens's "Ooh My Head" that was later included on *Physical Graffiti*.)

"It sounded good, and we went into the truck to hear it," Page told *Disc*'s Andrew Tyler. "We did about 30 seconds. Within 15 minutes, the whole framework for the rest had been written and recorded. That's quite raw, and those sorts of things are happening all the time. Whenever we get together, we come up with something."

"It's Been a Long Time"—or "Rock and Roll," as the song was eventually titled—was something of a departure for Led Zeppelin. For all that they adored early R&B and rockabilly—they'd often covered Elvis Presley's "That's Alright, Mama" live, for instance—they'd hitherto avoided that particular musical terrain on record. But the track makes a point, which was that Zeppelin was no less obsessed with '50s rock and roll than any of the other '70s acts (from Don McLean on "American Pie" to John Lennon on "Rock 'n' Roll") who paid homage to the stars of that era.

"The early rockabilly guitarists, like Cliff Gallup and Scotty Moore, were just as important to me as the blues guitarists," said Jimmy Page, whose collection of early Sun and rockabilly singles was rumored to rival even his collection of Aleister Crowley artifacts.

Plant, too, was something of an aficionado of American "oldies." The lyrics he wrote, virtually on the spot, amounted to a high-speed hymn of nostalgia, referencing the Diamonds, the Monotones, and the Drifters as he sought to rekindle the innocent magic of rock's early days. When interviewer Rick McGrath hung out with Zeppelin backstage in Vancouver at the end of the year, he watched the band "flailing away on acoustic guitars and loudly singing old rock hits like 'Save the Last Dance for Me' and 'The Bristol Stomp.'" Could one have imagined Grand Funk Railroad doing the same?

But even that isn't really the point of rock and roll. "Robert Plant sings *about* rock and roll," Chuck Eddy commented in his book *Stairway to Hell*, "but that's subsidiary: The sound *is* rock and roll, it rewrites the dictionary, curses anyone who won't accept the new way."

The unplugged side of Led Zeppelin, so powerfully in evidence on *Led Zeppelin III*, also made its presence felt at Headley Grange in January's 2-week creative blitz. Evenings were particularly conducive to quieter, more reflective songwriting. One night, after the others had retired to bed, Jimmy Page noticed the mandolin that John Paul Jones had acquired in America in 1969—and had taught himself to play, using only a copy of *Teach Yourself Bluegrass Mandolin*.

"I just picked up this mandolin and started playing a sequence," he told Stuart Grundy and John Tobler. "[It] probably consisted of the most basic chords on a mandolin, but from that I worked out the sequence to ['The Battle of Evermore']." Page told Dave Schulps that exactly the same thing had happened with the banjo part on *Led Zeppelin III*'s "Gallows Pole": "I'd never played one before. It was [Jonesy's] instrument again, I just picked it up and started playing, and it sort of worked. Started moving my fingers around until the chords sounded right, which is more or less the way I work on compositions anyway."

Although it was "my very first experiment with the [mandolin]"—whose tuning, moreover, was "totally different" from the guitar—Page claimed he was well-served by the basic fingerpicking technique he'd learned on London's folk circuit in the mid-'60s. "My fingerpicking," he said self-deprecatingly, "is a sort of cross between Pete Seeger, Earl Scruggs, and total incompetence."

Although Page admitted that "The Battle of Evermore" "sounded like a dance-around-the-maypole number," he claimed the song "wasn't purposely a 'Let's do a folksy number now.'" Initially, he said, "it sounded like an old English instrumental, and then it started to become a vocal."

As it happened, Page's chiming mandolin chords perfectly suited a song idea that Robert Plant had hatched at Bron-Yr-Aur, inspired by his ongoing immersion in both Tolkien's *Lord of the Rings* and the military history of the Middle Ages.

Picking up where *Led Zeppelin II*'s "Ramble On" left off, "The Battle of Evermore" references the Battle of Pelennor Fields from *The Return of the King*. The "Queen of Light" is Eowyn, the "Prince of Peace" Aragorn, the "Dark Lord" most likely Sauron. The namecheck for the Ringwraiths is the song's most explicit Tolkien connection. (Donald Swann, who had himself written the music for songs based on

The Lord of the Rings, opined that "Evermore" was "the best example of a contemporary song based on Tolkien's work I've heard.") But Plant also alludes to "the angels of Avalon," a nod to his fascination with English and Celtic mythology. In "The Battle of Evermore" he is particularly concerned with the border wars England waged against its Celtic neighbors, his sympathies clearly lying with the latter.

"Albion would have been a good place to be," Plant told *Record Mirror* in March 1972, "but that was England before it got messed up. You can live in a fairyland if you read enough books and if you're interested in as much history as I am—you know, the Dark Ages and all that."

The basic track for "The Battle of Evermore" was recorded quickly at the Grange, with the mandolin put through a Binson echo unit—a vintage Italian contraption with a small metal drum inside it. It was a device that would also come in handy for the epic "When the Levee Breaks."

Tolkien's influence is also present in "Misty Mountain Hop," the mountains in question featuring throughout *The Hobbit* and *The Lord of the Rings*. Arguably Plant's lyric draws allegorical parallels between hippies and the dwarves of *The Hobbit*: He was hardly the only hippie of his time to regard Tolkien as a sacred text of fantasy. The song concerns a drug bust, either in London or in San Francisco, and a consequent desire to flee to a place (the Misty

Mountains) *"where the spirits go now/Over the hills where the spirits fly. . . ."*

"Somebody once described me as the original hippie," Plant told *NME's* Charles Shaar Murray, "and that's because of the flowery lyrics, you know, and also because of the buzz we give out." At a New York press conference in 1970, Plant stated that what he wanted to get across in Led Zeppelin was "a message of enjoyment . . . for people to be happy."

When Cameron Crowe pointed out to Plant 4 years later that he'd been criticized for writing "dated flower-child gibberish," the singer responded testily. "The essence of the whole trip was the desire for peace and tranquility and an idyllic situation," he said. "That's all anybody could ever want, so how could it be 'dated flower-child gibberish'? If it is, then I'll just carry on being a dated flower child."

"Robert was more of an American type of peacenik than maybe the others were," says Henry Smith, himself an American. "He was more of a caring soul. I remember times that we would sit down in the '70s and go, 'Whatever happened to this peace-love generation? What made it stop in the United States and what made it stop in Europe?'"

As with "The Battle of Evermore," "Misty Mountain Hop" came together quickly at the Grange. The song's central riff was worked out by Jimmy Page—"I just came up with that on the spot," he remembered—before being developed one morning by John Paul

Jones, who'd woken earlier than his bandmates and plunked himself down at the electric piano. "Jonesy put the chords in for the chorus bit and that would shape up," Page recalled. "We used to work pretty fast. A lot of that would have been made up during the point of being at Headley."

An acoustic companion to "The Battle of Evermore," the beautiful "Going to California" contained no Tolkien references but was similarly born of what Page described as "a late-night guitar twiddle" at Headley. (The song's actual seed may have been planted in less bucolic circumstances, however. Plant introduced it thus at the Community Theater in Berkeley on September 14 that year: "This is a thing that got together . . . I was going to say in the Scottish highlands or the Welsh mountains, but I think it was something like the Gorham Hotel on West 37th Street.")

"That was the good thing about staying at [Headley Grange]," the guitarist said. "You didn't have anything like a snooker table or anything like that. No recreational purists at all. It was really good for discipline and getting on with the job. I suppose that's why a lot of these came at Headley Grange. For instance, "Going to California" and "Battle of Evermore" came out. But obviously then we got together and it was just away and afar, it was Jonesy on the mandolin, myself and Robert singing on it."

The trio in question gathered outside the next day,

the winter weather being unusually mild. "We did [the song] with all of us sitting outside on the grass playing mandolins and whatever else was around," Jones remembered. "At one point, you can actually hear an airplane going over, but we were always happy to leave that sort of thing in rather than lose a good take."

The premise of "Going to California" was simple: It was a love song to Los Angeles, or rather to the Golden State's more bucolic side. As Plant sang on "Stairway to Heaven," *there's a feeling I get when I look to the West. . . ."* Specifically, the song paid tribute to Joni Mitchell, the brilliant Canadian songstress who'd made Laurel Canyon her home early in 1968. *"Someone told me there's a girl out there,"* Robert Plant sang, *"With love in her eyes and flowers in her hair."* As the singer put it, "when you're in love with Joni Mitchell, you've really got to write about it now and again."

"That's the music that I play at home all the time, Joni Mitchell," Jimmy Page told Cameron Crowe in 1975. ". . . the main thing with Joni is that she's able to look at something that's happened to her, draw back and crystallize the whole situation, then write about it. She brings tears to my eyes, what more can I say?"

Robert Plant had mixed feelings about the "mellow" singer-songwriter scene that had blossomed in the LA canyons, not least because the laid-back, patched-denim troubadours within that scene looked on Led Zeppelin as bovine monsters of rock.

"The people who lived in Laurel Canyon avoided us," Plant said. "They kept clear because we were in the tackiest part of the Sunset Strip with tacky people like Kim Fowley and the GTOs. I wanted to know about the history of the Hollywood Argyles, and I would never have found that out at a candlelit dinner halfway up the Canyon."

Yet Plant had of course been a passionate devotee not only of Mitchell but of the Buffalo Springfield, whose Neil Young he had attempted to meet on an early Zeppelin visit to LA. "Robert desperately wanted to meet Neil," recalled Nancy Retchin, then a close friend of the Monkees. "Peter Tork said that CSNY was rehearsing at the Greek Theater and we could take Robert [around] there. Unfortunately on the day itself, I took mescalin, and I got so stoned that we ended up driving Robert in my mother's car all the way down to Watts. I'll never forget Robert yelling out of the car, *'Where's the Greek Theater?!,'* in this completely black neighborhood where nobody had ever heard of it."

For Plant, "the canyon scene was a continuation of the artistic will to create some sort of aesthetic and respectable role for pop music, so that there was an intention beyond 'Rock-a-Hula Baby.'" He none the less felt that "confessional" artists such as James Taylor had thrown the rock-and-roll baby out with the bathwater. "It's a shame that the whole solo singer-songwriter concept had to degenerate into that James Taylor thing of taking things so seriously," he told Nick Kent in December 1972. "Actually, this'll probably sound strange, but ultimately, I can envisage Pagey and myself ending up doing a whole Incredible String Band type of thing together. Very gentle stuff."

It doesn't get any gentler than "Going to California" in the Led Zeppelin songbook. Plant claimed that "for a mellow mood," it was his favorite Zeppelin song of all. "It's hard to say which single track pleases me most now, since there are so many moods to a day," he reflected. "'Going to California' is a really nice song. It's so simple, and the lyrics just fell out of my mouth." At the Berkeley show in September, he dedicated the song to "the days when things were really nice and simple, and everything was far out all the time."

Along with "Friends," "That's the Way," and others, "Going to California" duly became an integral part of the acoustic miniset the group incorporated into its live repertoire as a sort of musical sorbet between courses.

"I don't think the acoustic set was ever discussed as such," John Paul Jones said. "'Going to California' and 'That's the Way' were both written, rehearsed, and recorded just sitting in a semicircle, and it seemed an obvious way to present them live. It was also nice to have a rest, and it worked well for the dynamics."

The band, however, struggled to get the silence they wanted for their acoustic sets. On many occasions, Plant had to plead with audiences for a little quiet as they played. "You see, the essence of these numbers we wanna do now is silence," Plant declared before singing "That's the Way" and "Going to California" at the show in Rochester, New York. "The crying of voices doesn't really take us back to the Welsh mountains."

There was another acoustic interlude on Led Zeppelin's fourth album, of course. But little did Jimmy Page and Robert Plant guess, when it was completed one night at Headley Grange, that it would introduce the most famous epic in rock history.

5

THE TUNE WILL COME TO YOU AT LAST

"I DON'T want to tell you about it in case it doesn't come off," Jimmy Page told *NME* in April 1970. "It's an idea for a really long track on the next album. . . . We want to try something new with the organ and acoustic guitar building up and building up to the electric thing."

Having composed the intro for it at Bron-Yr-Aur in the spring of that year, Page continued to work on the "really long track" throughout 1970. Using an eight-track studio he'd installed in his Pangbourne boathouse, he spent many hours working out the different sections of what became "Stairway to Heaven," layering 6- and 12-string guitars with the aid of a recording unit called the New Vista.

"It was the deck from the Pye mobile that had been used to record things like the Who's *Live at Leeds*,"

Page recalled. "We'd used it to record our Albert Hall gig. I'd been fooling around with the acoustic guitar and came up with the different sections, which I married together. So I had the structure and then I ran it through Jonesy."

Although the band recorded an early instrumental version of the track at Island Studios in December 1970, "Stairway" at this point had no lyrics, nor was it structurally complete. Returning to it in Hampshire, Zeppelin slowly solved the problems it posed. "It may not make a lot of sense," Page remembered, "but it was quite a complicated song to actually get across to everybody."

Talking to Stuart Grundy and John Tobler in 1983, Page recalled the piecemeal process in more detail. "When we were recording it," he said, "there were little bits, little sections that I'd done, getting reference pieces down on cassette, and sometimes I referred back to them if I felt there was something that seemed right that could be included. I wanted to try this whole idea musically, this build toward a climax, with John Bonham coming in at a later point—an idea [that] I'd used before—to give it that extra kick."

The night after the mobile truck arrived at Headley Grange, Bonzo and Plant adjourned to the pub, leaving Page and Jones to write out the music for the complete version of the track. Bootleg tapes show the two men working out the transition from the song's bridge to its final solo, as well as Jones trying out keyboard parts on an electric piano.

"Both Jimmy and I were quite aware of the way a track should unfold and the various levels it would go through," Jones noted. "We were quite strong on form. . . . I suppose we were both quite influenced by classical music, and there's a lot of drama in the classical forms."

The following evening, with Jones and Bonham taking a night off—driving to London for a party at the Speakeasy club—Page and Plant sat together in Headley Grange's drawing room. "Jimmy and I just sat by the fire; it was a remarkable setting," Plant recalled. "I mean, Hawkwind was probably humming in the background." As Page picked out the intro chords, Plant's flagging inspiration was suddenly revived.

"I was holding a pencil and paper, and for some reason I was in a very bad mood," Plant recalled. "Then all of a sudden, my hand was writing out the words, *'There's a lady who's sure all that glitters is gold/And she's buying a stairway to heaven.'* I just sat there and looked at the words and then I almost leapt out of my seat."

The next day, with the rhythm section returned, more of the song's lyrics tumbled out of Plant as he sat listening to Page, Jones, and Bonham play. "We were going over and over it from the beginning to the end quite a few times, with Robert sitting on the stool," said Page. "[We] were all so inspired by how the song could come out—with the building passages and all of those possibilities—that [he] suddenly burst out with the lyrics. Then we all threw in ideas— things such as Bonzo not coming in until the song was well underway to create a change of gear—and the song and the arrangement just came together."

"Stairway" ran aground only in one spot in the song. "For some unknown reason, Bonzo couldn't get the timing on the 12-string intro to the solo," Page told Dave Schulps. "Apart from that, it flowed very quickly. By the time we'd gone through it a few times, Robert was obviously penciling down words. About 75 to 80 percent of the words he wrote on the spot. Amazing, really. In other words, he didn't go away and think about it, or have to sort of ponder and ponder and ponder. . . ."

"I have an image of Robert sitting on a radiator," said Richard Cole. "He was working out the words to 'Stairway' while John Paul pulled out a recorder. Whenever they went into prerecording, John Paul would come down with a carload of instruments, usually different acoustic instruments."

"We always had a lot of instruments lying around, so I picked up a bass recorder and played along with Jimmy," Jones recalled. "Later at Island, I multi-tracked the recorders to get it right."

"It was done very quickly," Plant said of "Stairway." "It was a very fluid, unnaturally easy track.

There was something pushing it, saying, 'You guys are okay, but if you want to do something timeless, here's a wedding song for you.'"

A wedding song "Stairway to Heaven" is not, but a song about real versus fake spirituality it does appear to be. Although Plant has always stressed the ambiguity of his lyric, he has also said that the lady of the song's opening line is "a woman getting everything she wanted without giving anything back"—someone for whom the stairway in question is a materialistic fast track to spiritual grace. The idea that you can "buy" some ascension to Nirvana would naturally be abhorrent to a "dated flower child" such as Plant.

"It's like she can have anything forever, so long as she doesn't have to think about it," the singer has said. "[But] good will prevail over the whole thing and logic will reign and all that. . . ." For Plant, "Stairway to Heaven" was about "potential optimism." "Lyrically it's saying that if you hold tight, you can make it all right," he explained. Introducing the song at Madison Square Garden in *The Song Remains the Same*, he announced that it was "a song of hope."

Given Plant's interest in magic and mythology— he'd been poring over books by British antiquarian Lewis Spence, including *The Magic Arts in Celtic Britain*—the musical setting Page and Jones had devised for the song made it perfect for a lyric that reads like a fairy tale. The imprint of American blues had never been so absent in a Led Zeppelin song. "It's . . . incredibly English," Plant admitted. "It sounds almost medieval. At times it sounds like, you know, you want to have swirling mists."

"Robert is just very much in sympathy with the vibe of my music," Page told Mick Houghton in 1976. "There's a certain amount of discussion, but usually it's just there naturally. I'm sure I could write down on a piece of paper how I visualized a piece of music before Robert writes the lyrics, and they would match up. It comes back to the chemistry of the group." Page told Houghton that after Plant had written "Stairway to Heaven," "there was just no point in my writing any more lyrics since I wasn't going to top anything like that." Significantly, the song's lyrics were reproduced on the sleeve of the album, the first occasion on which any Zeppelin lyrics had appeared on an album cover.

"I always knew [Robert] would be [the main lyricist]," Page told Dave Schulps, "but I knew at that point that he'd sort of proved it to himself, and he could sort of get into something more profound than just, say, subjective things . . . and I was relieved because it gave me more of a chance to get on with just doing the music."

"It just knows that there's so many different twists and turns to everyone's life," Plant said of "Stairway." "If you keep a diary or you express yourself in any way, you refer to it. Writing songs kind of tells you how you were at the time—at least how you were projecting yourself at various points in time."

The "medieval" feel of Page's delicate intro is underscored by the recorders that John Paul Jones played alongside him, transporting us as they do to some hazy pastoral scene out of, say, Edmund Spenser's epic poem *The Faerie Queene*. Susan Fast also notes "traces of 16th/early 17th century Tudor music" in the chords and arrangement.

When Page brings in his 12-string electric, however, the feel shifts instantly, as though ushering us out of the misty, distant past into the amplified present. The song thus begins the ascent to its frenzied climax, complete with the passionate solo—over chords borrowed from Bob Dylan's "All Along the Watchtower"—that Page only managed to nail in an overdub at Island Studios, having abandoned the attempt at Headley Grange.

"He was trying to get the guitar solo for 3 or 4 hours," Andy Johns recalled of the session at Headley. "It started to worry me because time after time he would say, 'What do you think?' and I'd say, 'Not bad,' meaning it needed work. Eventually, when he asked me yet again, I sort of cracked and said, 'You're making me paranoid!' And he said, 'No, you're making *me* paranoid!' and we had a big argument. It made me realize he was as insecure as anyone."

Not that Page was any less nervous when the time came to record "Stairway" at Island in early February. "I get terrible studio nerves," he admitted in December 1971. "Even when I've worked the whole thing out beforehand at home, I get terribly nervous playing it—particularly when it's something that turned out to be a little above my normal capabilities. My [nerve] goes." To Ritchie Yorke, he confessed, the stress was such that "I might as well be back years ago making all those dreadful studio records."

Watching Page struggle in the big Studio One room on Basing Street was a young tape-operator named Richard Digby-Smith. "Page was playing acoustic guitar sat at the front with four tall baffles that completely enclosed him," Digby-Smith recalled. "There were no windows at all, and you couldn't see in or out; it was just like a little square. Jones was to the right of him playing Moog bass, which was the industry standard at the time. You know, it was a keyboard, Moog keyboard bass. Bonzo just sat at the back, you know, waiting for that bit where he comes pounding in. . . ." To Digby-Smith's ears, it sounds "faultless" from beginning to end.

"They run up the stairs for the playback," the former tape-op continued. "Sounds wonderful. Bonham says, 'That's it, then!' But Pagey's quiet. He's a man of few words anyway. His hand's on his chin, he's going 'Mmmm, mmmm'—you never knew what he was thinking. So Bonham looks at him and says, 'What's up?' And Page says he's convinced that they have a better take in them.

"Well, Bonham's not best pleased. 'This always happens—we get a great take and you want to do it again.' They go back down. Bonzo grabs his sticks, huffing, puffing, muttering, 'One more take and that's it!' He waits and waits until he makes his grand entrance and, of course, when the drums come in, if you thought the one before was good, this one is just explosive. And when they play it back, Bonham looks at Jimmy, like, 'You're always right, you bastard.'"

When John Paul Jones had overdubbed three recorder parts (baritone, tenor, soprano) for the song's intro, it was finally time for Page to record his solo. "He did three takes," Digby-Smith said. "He didn't use headphones; he monitored the backing tracks through speakers, which was how the classical solo-ists who used that studio did it."

The sight of Page leaning against a big orange speaker, cigarette dangling from his mouth as he played, was one Digby-Smith never forgot. "We played him back through them as loud as possible," the former tape-op remembered. "He just leaned up against the speakers with his ear virtually pressed against them . . . and rattled out that solo. He was the epitome of cool."

"I winged it every time," Page claimed of the three "quite different" solos he played. "I'd prepared the overall structure of the guitar parts but not the actual notes. I did all those guitars on it; I just built them up.

That was the beginning of my building up harmonized guitars properly."

Instead of playing the solo on a Gibson Les Paul, the preferred Page guitar of the time, Jimmy opted for a 1958 Fender Telecaster of the type he'd routinely played in the Yardbirds. "I steered away from the Les Paul because it was all sort of there giving it all to you, the sustain and stuff. . . ." Instead, one can hear Page almost fighting with the guitar, strangling it to get the notes he needs. In March 2006, the readers of *Total Guitar* magazine voted "Stairway" the best air guitar solo of all time, beating solos by Hendrix, Clapton, and Brian May to the honor.

When it was finally completed, "Stairway to Heaven" was every bit the milestone Page had hoped for—the pomp-rock climax of Led Zeppelin's ambition at that point in its career. "That really sums it all up," he told Stuart Grundy and John Tobler. "It's just a glittering thing, and it was put together in such a way as to bring in all the fine points, musically, of the band in its construction." He added that he would "have to do a lot of hard work before I can get anywhere near those stages of consistent, total brilliance again."

While Zeppelin recorded several other multi-section epics through the '70s—"No Quarter," "The Song Remains the Same," "Kashmir," "In the Light," "Achilles' Last Stand," "Carouselambra"—the band never topped this Everest of progressive rock. Live, "Stairway" became the centerpiece of Zeppelin's act, especially after Jimmy Page acquired his famous double-necked (12-string and 6-string) Gibson SG in order to play it.

"There's this fanfare toward the solo," he recalled, "and Robert comes in after that with this tremendous vocal thing. At the time, there were quite a few guitars overlaid on that, and I must admit I thought—I knew—it was going to be very difficult to do it on stage, but we had to do it, we really wanted to do it, and I got a double-necked guitar to approach it." (Jones, meanwhile, was forced in concert to reproduce the three multitracked recorders on the "Stairway" intro on a Mellotron that recalled the Moody Blues' "Nights in White Satin.")

"Stairway" was received enthusiastically almost from the day of its live debut at Belfast's Ulster Hall on March 5, 1971. In America, one show in particular—at the LA Forum on August 21—convinced Page that the song would become a classic.

"It's a long track when you think about it," he said. "You know how difficult it is when you go and hear a concert and hear a number from a band for the first time, and that's quite a long time to concentrate on something. I remember we got a standing ovation from a considerable amount of that audience, and we went, 'Wow!' [We] didn't realize that people would latch on to it, but from testing the gauge of it like that, it was an early reaction. We thought, 'That's great, fabulous.'"

But if Page saw "Stairway" as a classic—"an apex, lyrically"—the song's lyricist was more diffident as to its qualities. "I don't consider there was anything particularly special about it," Plant said almost churlishly. "The only thing that gives it any staying power at all is its ambiguity."

"It was a nice, pleasant, well-meaning, naive little song, very English," the singer added in 1988. "It's not the definitive Zeppelin song. 'Kashmir' is. I'd break out in hives if I had to sing 'Stairway to Heaven' in every show." The singer claimed he'd only agreed to perform it at the Atlantic anniversary show that year "because I'm an old softie and it was a way of saying thank you . . . but no more of 'Stairway to Heaven' for me." (Plant did, however, perform an acoustic version of the song on Japanese TV when he and Page were promoting *No Quarter: Jimmy Page and Robert Plant Unledded* in 1994.)

Jimmy Page has long been the song's most strident champion. Where Plant refused to sing the song after the band's demise, the guitarist continued to perform it as an instrumental. In 1983 and 1984, he concluded a series of charity concerts with "Stairway," delighting fans who could have cared less about Plant's absence.

The critics have tended to take Plant's side, however. Ever since Lester Bangs described "Stairway to Heaven" as "a thicket of misbegotten mush," the song has been regarded as—at best—a colossal joke, a pseudoclassical epic that's impossible to take seriously.

When, in the film *Wayne's World*, Mike Myers enters a guitar shop and observes a sign that says, simply, "NO STAIRWAY," he is making fun of the countless Page wannabes who have lurked in every suburb and small town in middle America. The Stonehenge-with-dwarves scene in *This Is Spinal Tap* was in part a lampoon of Zeppelin's medievalist pretensions. Twenty-two spoof versions of "Stairway," including a hit rendition by Rolf Harris, appeared on an Australian compilation in 1993. The Butthole Surfers titled a 1988 album *Hairway to Steven*.

True, "Stairway" became *the* template for the slow-building, multipart "power ballad" that came to grace the repertoire of every hard rock and AOR band in America. But its status as rock's ultimate "long track" makes it hard to hear properly, obscuring both its beauty and its power.

"Stairway" has also been tainted by the risible charges of satanic allusion that have accompanied Jimmy Page throughout his career. In 1981, for instance, a Michigan minister named Michael Mills claimed that phrases such as "Master Satan" and "serve me" were embedded in the song's grooves.

Page had little truck with such interpretations. For him, as with all of Led Zeppelin's music, the track was first and foremost about feeling. "Those records were extremely emotional," he said. "If that's the way they interpret it, if that deep intense emotion was satanic, then they've got no idea what we're about."

Page may have regarded "Stairway to Heaven" as the "apex" of Led Zeppelin's career to date, but it was the 7-minute "When the Levee Breaks" that represented for him the "high point" of the group's fourth album.

Written by blues singer Memphis Minnie and her husband, Kansas Joe McCoy, shortly before they left Tennessee for Chicago in the economically disastrous year of 1929, "Levee" told of the devastating floods that had swamped the south in the '20s. *"Cryin' won't help you, prayin' won't do you no good,"* Minnie had sung. *"When the levee breaks, mama, you got to move."*

For Led Zeppelin, "When the Levee Breaks" stood with "Black Dog" as a necessary counterweight to the fourth album's more ethereal moments. Swampy, almost grungily primeval, "Levee" was a second dose of heavy blues that returned the band to their 12-bar roots. Placing "Black Dog" and "Levee" at each end of the record was surely intentional: Not for nothing did Jimmy Page describe "When the Levee Breaks" as "sucking you into the source." (Zeppelin matched the sheer dread of "Levee" only one more time, on *Physical Graffiti*'s astounding "In My Time of Dying." But they stayed truer to their blues animus than the Rolling Stones did: There was nothing like "In My Time of Dying" on *It's Only Rock 'n Roll* or *Black and Blue*.)

"The denouement of [the album] is not some misty peak," wrote Erik Davis, who sees "Levee" as "Zeppelin's definitive blues song on record . . . Instead we fall away from myth and return to the root, to matter, to a dirge of the earth."

"If 'Stairway to Heaven' is how you get there," noted Chuck Eddy, "'When the Levee Breaks' is how you get back." "Levee," said Eddy, is the Stairway to hell.

Zeppelin took Minnie's Delta woes and turned them into a massive, driving beast of a track, Page's grinding slide riffs meshing with Plant's squalling harmonica and forced forward by the mightiest drum sound ever captured on tape. The brutal, elemental drone of "When the Levee Breaks"—rivaled only by the awesome "Kashmir," recorded at Headley Grange 3 years later—never ceases to astonish.

The ambience of Headley Grange had everything to do with the song's power. "We tried to record it in a studio before we got to Headley Grange, and it sounded flat," Page recalled. "But once we got the drum sound at Headley Grange, it was like, 'Boom!'"

It was actually a new Ludwig kit, delivered to the Grange halfway through the sessions, that Bonham played on "Levee." "It must have been in the hands of the gods, really," Page said. "We would say, 'Wait until the drum kit arrives and everything is going to be fine.'"

According to Andy Johns, while Page, Plant, and

Jones took a pub break, he and John Bonham set the new kit up in the hallway. "We'd been working on another song, and there was a lot of leakage from the drums," John Paul Jones recalled. "So we moved [them] out into the hall where there's a big stairwell."

Johns then hung two ambient Beyer M160 stereo microphones over the kit, one 10 feet up, the other about 20. "[Bonzo's] kit was very well-balanced internally," the engineer remembered. "Each drum's volume was consistent with the others. In the truck, I put him into two channels and compressed the drums." Johns then ran the resulting signal through the Binson echo unit he'd used on "The Battle of Evermore," the effect instantly blowing his mind.

"I remember sitting there thinking it sounded utterly amazing," Johns remembered. "I ran out of the truck and said, 'Bonzo, you gotta come in and hear this!' And he came in and shouted, 'Whoa, that's it! That's what I've been hearing!'"

By this, one can only assume Bonham meant what he'd been hearing in his head all through the sessions—like some Platonic ideal of how hard rock drums should sound. The primordial thwack of the "Levee" beat, with its fat, booming echo, was almost industrial in density—in Lester Bangs's words "a great groaning, oozing piece of sheer program music." No wonder the band delayed the entrance of Plant's vocal for almost a minute and a half.

"There was a secret to it [that] we just stumbled

across, really," Plant said. "[It] was just one [sic] microphone—and the revelation of finding out that that one microphone did more than about 35 in a studio [that] set the mood. It was enthusiasm."

"I had a whole concept of how this thing was going to end up," Page said. "But it just so happened that we put a mike into the hallway, which—as it was a three-story house with the stairs going all the way up—had all this beautiful space. So, on the second landing was just a stereo mike, and the sound was just phenomenal. That was it—it was going to be *the* drum song. As soon as it was set up, it was the one we went for, and it worked."

"Bonzo started playing and we said, 'Jesus, will you listen to that sound,'" John Paul Jones recalled. "Then we started the riff and that's how the song came about—through experimentation."

Jones, Plant, and Page were particularly struck by the fact that Johns and Bonham had dispensed with a separate mike for the bass drum. "We could have used a separate [mike], but we didn't need to," Page told *Guitar World*. "[Bonzo's] kick sound was that powerful. And his playing was not in his arms, it was all in his wrist action. Frightening! I still do not know how he managed to get so much level out of a kit." For Page, nobody other than Bonham could have created what he described as "that sex groove."

The influence of Bonham's groove on "When the Levee Breaks" has carried all the way through to hip-hop. Sampled by artists as different as the Beastie Boys ("Rhymin' and Stealin"), Dr Dre ("Lyrical Gangbang"), and Ice T ("Midnight"), the opening four bars of "Levee"—Bonham unaccompanied, laying down that on-the-beat funk pulse—have become part of rap's fabric. (Similarly, *Physical Graffiti*'s epic "Kashmir"—also recorded at Headley Grange—has been sampled on Schooly D's "Signifying Rapper" and Puff Daddy's "Come to Me.")

"I think we set a trend with all of this," Page told Stuart Grundy and John Tobler. "That whole drum sound and all this ambience is now captured digitally in the machine. Where we would do it that way, you've now got it in machines."

Machines played their part in the making of "When the Levee Breaks," with the addition of backward echo to both the guitar and harmonica tracks. "'When the Levee Breaks' was probably the most subtle thing on there, as far as the production aspect [goes]," Page told Dave Schulps, "because each 12-bar has got something totally new about it, although at first it may not be apparent. It's got different effects on it, which now people have heard a number of times but which at the time hadn't been used before: phased vocals and harmonica solos backward . . . a lot of backward echo."

Backward echo was a gimmick Page had pioneered on the Yardbirds's "Ten Little Indians," and now he wanted to create a kind of sonic whirlpool with the effect. "That was done at Island," Andy Johns recalled. "I put the harp through an old Fender Princeton with tremolo and miked it up."

"A lot of times, we'd leave Jimmy alone to do his layering and his overdubs," said Richard Cole. "You'd leave on a Friday afternoon, and then when you turned up on a Monday morning, you'd hear something completely different."

"All the overdubs were done at Island," Page told Dave Schulps, "because the truck wasn't too together for too many overdubs. I worked quite a lot on the overdubs on those things. 'Stairway' [has got] quite a few guitars on it, and 'Four Sticks' was another one, with loads of chiming guitars and things that all had to be done in the studio."

Finishing touches were put to other Headley Grange tracks at Island. First and foremost were a number of guitar overdubs—most crucially on "Black Dog," which Page had already earmarked as an opening track that would be as strong as "Good Times, Bad Times," "Whole Lotta Love," and "Immigrant Song."

The guitars on "Black Dog," triple-tracked and plugged straight into the mixing desk without being amplified, have the fat, glossy timbre of synthesizers. "We put my Les Paul through a direct box, and from there into a mike channel," Page confided to *Guitar World*. "We used the mike amp of the mixing board to get distortion. Then we ran it through two Urie 1176 Universal compressors in series. Then each line was triple-tracked. Curiously, I was listening to that track when we were reviewing the tapes, and the guitars almost sound like an analog synthesizer."

"[It] was a trick I learned from Bill Halverson, who worked with Buffalo Springfield," Andy Johns told Robert Godwin. "The only problem was that the second Jimmy would stop playing, [and] a huge amount of background noise would come surging up, which we had to try and fix in the mix. At the time, I thought it was damn fine and a novel effect."

To Page, the guitars on "Four Sticks" were almost as important as those on "Black Dog." "I can see certain milestones along the way like 'Four Sticks,' in the middle section of that," he told Steven Rosen. "The sound of those guitars—that's where I'm going."

The song, long the least popular track on ⚡️🜪🕸️🕉️ but a vital influence on LA band Jane's Addiction, had eventually come into its own at Headley Grange, but only when John Bonham attempted it again with the four drumsticks of the title. As with the perverse rhythms of "Black Dog," Zeppelin here strayed into the realm of the unfeasible, fluctuating between five- and six-beat meters.

"I had real problems working out where the beat should go," said John Paul Jones, who'd fallen ill for a couple of days and left the others to get on with things. "Rhythmically, it was quite unusual, but I was the only one in the band who could do that because of my background as an arranger."

⚡️🜪🕸️🕉️

"It was two takes, but that was because it was physically impossible for him to do another," Jimmy Page said of John Bonham's drumming on the track. "I couldn't get that to work until we tried to record it a few times, and I just didn't know what it was and I still wouldn't have known what it was. We probably would have kicked the track out." After much fuming and cussing, said Page, "Bonzo . . . just picked up the four sticks and that was it."

At Island, John Paul Jones overdubbed the VCR synthesizer solo on the song's second middle-eight section. By the time it was complete, "Four Sticks" just about worked as an exotic oddity, its crabbed Oriental feel making it a missing link between "Friends" and "Kashmir." (When Page and Plant journeyed to India the following year, they recorded versions of both "Friends" and "Four Sticks" with members of the Bombay Symphony Orchestra.)

"It was a bastard to mix," said Andy Johns. "When I originally recorded the basic tracks, I compressed the drums. Then when I went to mix, I couldn't make it work. I did it five or six times." It didn't help that a quarter-inch tape of the track was missing.

If "Four Sticks" felt like a milestone to Page, the fourth album as a whole gave him immense satisfaction as a guitarist. He told Steven Rosen that "as far as consistency goes and as far as the quality of playing on a whole album," ⚭⚭⚭ was his greatest achievement.

"My vocation is more in composition, really, than in anything else," he told Rosen. "Building up harmonies. Using the guitar, orchestrating the guitar like an army—a guitar army. I think that's where it's at, really, for me. I'm talking about actual orchestration in the same way you'd orchestrate a classical piece of music. Instead of using brass and violins, you treat the guitars with synthesizers or other devices; give them different treatments, so that they have enough frequency range and scope and everything to keep the listener as totally committed to it as the player is. It's a difficult project, but it's one that I've got to do."

The post-Headley sessions at Island witnessed another crucial overdub, this time on "The Battle of Evermore." "It was really more of a playlet than a song," Robert Plant said of the track in April 1972. "After I wrote the lyrics, I realized I needed another, completely different voice, as well as my own, to give that song its full impact."

Sandy Denny, late of folk-rockers Fairport Convention and about to part company with her subsequent group Fotheringay, was Plant's "favorite singer out of all the British girls that ever were." He decided she would be the perfect vocal foil for "Evermore." "I approached Sandy . . . and she was up for it," he recalled. "I don't think it took more than 45 minutes. I showed her how to do the long '*Oooooh, dance in the dark*' so there'd be a vocal tail-in. It was perfect against my bluesy thing."

To Plant, Denny "answered back as if she was the pulse of the people on the battlements." He saw her as playing the role of the town crier, "urging the people to throw down their weapons." Denny claimed she'd left the studio feeling hoarse. "Having someone outsing you is a horrible feeling, wanting to be strongest yourself," she told Barbara Charone in 1973.

"For me to sing with Sandy was great," Plant said, looking back on the session in 2005. "Sandy and I were friends, and it was the most obvious thing to ask her to sing on 'The Battle.' If it suffered from a naivety and tweeness—I was only 23—it makes up for it in the cohesion of the voices and the playing."

By the time Zeppelin had finished at Island, they had 14 tracks in the can. These included tracks from earlier sessions, as well as the songs begun or developed at Headley Grange. The option to make their fourth album a double was finally discarded, however. "We have enough here for two albums, but we won't put out a double album," Page announced. "I think people can appreciate a single album better."

The group had also decided to break with tradition, title-wise. "This next album won't be called *Led Zeppelin IV*," Plant told *Disc*'s Caroline Boucher in February. "We'll think of something else."

From the second Bron-Yr-Aur stay to the final session at Island, the entire process of recording Led Zeppelin's fourth album had taken little more than 2 months—with a Christmas break included. After the week of rehearsals at Headley Grange, the band had spent only a further 6 days there with the Stones's mobile unit.

"Looking back, I suppose what we really needed was at least 2 weeks solid with the truck," Page admitted. "But as it turned out, we actually had only about 6 days. Usually, we need a full week to get everything out of our system and to get used to the facilities."

On February 9, Page and Andy Johns packed up the tapes and flew to Los Angeles to mix the album. Little did they know how long the process was going to take.

6

PRAYIN' WON'T DO YOU NO GOOD

"THE MOUNTAINS and the canyons start to tremble and shake," Robert Plant sings on "Going to California." *"The children of the sun begin to wake ..."*

As Jimmy Page and Andy Johns landed at LAX on Tuesday, February 9, 1971, they felt the tremors of the Sylmar earthquake that shook Los Angeles at 2 minutes past 6:00 that morning. "As we were coming down the escalators into the main terminal, there was a slight earthquake," Page recalled. "In fact, it was quite big. It cracked one of the dams there in San Diego, and in the hotel before going to the studio, you could feel the bed shaking. I thought, 'Well, here we go.'" It was an omen of sorts for the shaky experience that lay ahead.

Johns had used Sunset Sound studios before, having mixed an album there by a group called Sky. But his ulterior motive for mixing in LA was to progress a relationship he'd begun on an earlier visit. Page, for his part, was only too eager to resume relations with pretty Miss Pamela, the GTOs member who'd been his LA consort of choice. Keeping an eye on both men was Peter Grant, who'd flown out to join them.

The moment Johns sat down at Sunset Sound, however, it was clear to him that the monitors had been changed. The sound in the room was very different from the one he remembered. Moving to a different room within the complex wasn't a solution, either. "We should have just gone home," Johns admitted later. "But I didn't want to and I don't think Jimmy did, either. We were having a good time, you know?"

For several days, the engineer and the guitarist labored over the fourth-album mix. "We wasted a week [messing] around," Page grouched after the fact. "It had sounded all right to me, but the speakers were lying. It wasn't the balance; it was the actual sound that was on the tape. All I can put it down to was the fact that the speakers in LA and the monitoring system in that room were just very bright—and they lied. It wasn't the true sound."

Johns confessed that mixing was "still a bit of a mystery" to him and Page: "We were really young. We never took tapes home to listen to or we might have known."

One Sunset Sound mix, however, turned out to be a winner. "One of my favorite mixes is at the end of

'When the Levee Breaks,'" Page told *Guitar World*, "when everything starts moving around except for the voice, which stays stationary." Page was particularly proud of the panning and "extreme positioning" he and Johns achieved in the song's final 2 minutes, even if this can be properly appreciated only on high-quality headphones.

"At the end of it, where we've got the whole works going on this fade, it doesn't actually fade," Jimmy said. "As we finished it, the whole effects start to spiral; all the instruments are now spiraling. This was very difficult to do in those days, I can assure you. With the mixing and the voice remaining constant in the middle. You hear everything turning right around." Perhaps this was what Page meant by the phrase "sucking you into the source."

After they'd finished the mix, Johns's older brother Glyn—who'd worked on the first Zeppelin album—dropped by for a listen. "We were really excited and told him, 'You've got to listen to this,'" Page recalled. "Glyn listened and just said, 'Hmm, you'll never be able to cut it. It'll never work.' And he walked out. Wrong again, Glyn. He must have been seething with envy."

Glyn Johns would not have been seething with envy when his brother brought the mixes back to London. "When we got back, the other guys wanted to hear the mixes," Johns recalled. "We went into Olympic for a playback, which was another mistake.

The only things that sound good in that room is stuff that's been recorded there."

"[Jimmy] brought the tapes back and they sounded terrible, so we had to start mixing all over again," Plant told *Disc* in November. "The sound of the mixing room that Andy Johns took Jimmy to was really [useless]." Johns admitted that he and Page "crouched in the corner really embarrassed" as Plant, Jones, and Bonham listened in stunned disbelief. "I thought my number was up," Johns later said. "But the others seemed to look to Jimmy, even though it was just as much my fault." It was the last time Johns worked with the band.

Having originally intended to release the album in March, Led Zeppelin now had to put it on hold while they undertook a short UK tour that Peter Grant had booked. Remixing would be impossible before April.

Grant, eager to bolster the band's UK fan base in the face of ongoing resentment at their focus on the US market, had been looking into the possibility of staging two London concerts: one at Waterloo Station, the other at the Oval cricket club. In the event, neither of these ambitious events panned out.

Instead, with a view to getting back to their roots, Grant hatched the concept of playing a select number of smaller venues around Britain. In part, this was a thank-you to fans and promoters, in part a platform for road-testing the new songs, and in part a silencing of rumors that Zeppelin was planning to split.

"The boys came to me after Christmas and talked about their next tour," Grant told *Melody Maker*'s Chris Welch. "We decided to do the clubs and forget about the bread and the big concert halls. We're going to restrict prices to about 12 bob [shillings] a ticket. When I rang the Marquee, the manager refused to believe it was me offering him Led Zeppelin, so he had to call me back to be convinced."

The "Back to the Clubs" UK tour began at Belfast's Ulster Hall on March 5. Here, against a backdrop of sectarian violence and rioting, Zeppelin played "Stairway to Heaven" live for the first time. "'Stairway to Heaven' is a good representation of what we're doing now," Plant told *Melody Maker*'s Chris Welch, who'd flown to Belfast to see the show. "There are different moods to the song, which lasts 10 or 12 minutes." Plant said there was "a kind of instant excitement" about playing live again.

The English leg of the tour began at Leeds University on March 9, continuing with shows in Canterbury, Southampton, Bath, Stoke, Newcastle, Manchester, Birmingham, Nottingham, and (on March 23) London, where hundreds of fans lined up around the block for tickets—most doomed to be disappointed. As for Zeppelin themselves, "Back to the Clubs" was a well-meaning experiment they did not repeat again.

"They may have liked that closeness with the audience," said Richard Cole, "but I don't think they were really that enamored of the backstage facilities after all the stadium tours they'd done. It wasn't that they were people who really had anything flashy in their dressing rooms—they had fuck apart from drinks and sandwiches—but the dressing rooms were so small, it was like, 'We're not gonna do *this* in a hurry again.' I think they'd forgotten what it was like."

On April Fool's Day, the group recorded a session for John Peel's BBC show *Rock Hour* at the Paris studios on London's Lower Regent Street. "Stairway," now more honed in its live arrangement, was performed along with "Black Dog," the latter prefaced by the intro to *Led Zeppelin III*'s "Out on the Tiles." Introducing the set's acoustic segment—"Going to California" and "That's the Way"—Plant muttered that "this is the time where we like to have a cup of tea, so I think we'd better sit down instead." "Whole Lotta Love" and "Dazed and Confused" were wheeled out, together with a covers medley that included John Lee Hooker's "Boogie Chillun" and Elvis Presley's "That's Alright, Mama." The rapturously received set concluded with *Led Zeppelin II*'s "Thank You."

By mid-April, Jimmy Page was back at Olympic and Island, working on new mixes for the fourth album. (All mixes on the record were credited as being "with Andy Johns" except "The Battle of Evermore," which credited George Chkiantz.) Due to further live bookings, the mixing process continued all the way into June. "It's that long dragging-out thing of mixing a lot of the tracks," Robert Plant told *Sounds*'s Steve Peacock. "It's a drag having to do it twice, but we're coming to the tail end of it now."

It didn't help that Led Zeppelin was meticulous to the point of anal retentiveness. "We used to spend hours, weeks, months sometimes in one room," Plant says. "All going, 'Mmm . . . no . . . let's just close the gap between those two tracks a bit more. . . .' All that nuancing."

Plant was nonetheless beginning to feel excited about the finished album. In the interview with Steve Peacock, conducted in late June, the singer described the LP. "Out of the lot, I should think there are about three or four mellow things," he said. "But there's also some nice strong stuff, some really . . . we don't say 'heavy,' do we? Well, I don't know whether we do. But it's strong stuff and exciting, and the flame is really burning higher and higher."

Looking back almost 35 years later, Plant could still take great pride in the record. "I think [it] was beautifully written in most areas," he told *Uncut*'s Nigel Williamson. "It wasn't overstated. It was crafted."

"We were really playing properly," Jimmy Page told Dave Schulps. "The different writing departures that we'd taken, and the cottage, and the spontaneity aspect, plus things that we'd written at home . . . really came across in their best . . . their most disciplined form."

Even now, the saga of ☙❀❦❋ wasn't quite finished. "There was a holdup about pressings, and whether the masters would stand up to how many pressings," Plant recalled. "The whole story of the fourth album reads like a nightmare." Finally, early in July 1971, the mixed tapes were delivered to Soho's Trident Studios for mastering. The fourth Led Zeppelin album was finished.

Except, of course, that it wasn't. There were still decisions to be made about the album's presentation—about its title, its sleeve, and its marketing.

The album's title was a thorny issue for the band. So angry were they at their treatment by the rock press that they wanted the LP to make a kind of anti-statement. "Names, titles, and things like that don't mean a thing," remark Jimmy Page. "What does 'Led Zeppelin' mean? It doesn't mean a thing. What matters is our music. If we weren't playing good music, nobody would care what we call ourselves. If the music was good, we could call ourselves the Cabbage and still get across to our audience."

Following the lead of the Beatles's deliberately nonhyped "White Album" in 1968—and perhaps influenced by the Byrds's *(Untitled)* (1970)—Zeppelin decided their fourth album simply wouldn't *have* a title. As Page remembered it, "I put it to everybody else that it might be a good idea to put out something [that] was totally anonymous." Moreover, the sleeve would feature no words of any kind. "We wanted a cover with no writing on it," Robert Plant said. "No company symbols or anything. The hierarchy of the record business isn't into the fact that covers are important to a band's image."

"When you haven't put out an album for a year, and there's this huge enigma that's blown up, and then you put out an album with no title whatsoever," Jimmy Page said, "some people would consider that to be suicide. But the whole thing had to be done to satisfy our own minds after all the crap that had gone down in the newspapers—and still does."

By "all the crap," Page meant the charges of hype that had accompanied Led Zeppelin from the onset of their career. For the group, the underselling of their fourth album was an opportunity to make a point. "There aren't any photographs of the band members to be found anywhere on the double jacket or its inner sleeve," American critic Ron Ross wrote in 1975. "No title, no pix, no gimmicks. Whatever one decided to call Led Zeppelin, a 'hype' was never appropriate."

"I think the genius of Jimmy Page that people are always missing is the idea of the anti-establishment 'punk' things that he was doing," said Jack White. "Things like releasing records with no information and no writing on the cover. I mean, that's pretty bold. Not releasing singles. Not doing interviews. All those things were pretty punk, man. A lot more punk than the Sex Pistols signing a contract in front of Buckingham Palace."

Instead of a title, Zeppelin chose to print four runic

symbols on the album's label, as well as on the spine of its cover. The "name" of the band's fourth album was, literally, the symbols they individually chose to represent themselves. "I think *Four Symbols* at the time was how it was referred to by us," Page told the BBC. "But it is runes, yeah, runes. [Though] I don't think we used to refer to it as the runes album ourselves."

The runes in question were symbols pictured in Rudolph Koch's *The Book of Signs*, a typically esoteric volume owned by Page. "[Jimmy] showed me this book he had," John Paul Jones remembered, "and said we should all choose a symbol from the book to represent each one of us." Later, after they'd picked their symbols, Jones and John Bonham learned that Page and Plant had had their runes custom-designed. "Typical, really," huffed Jones.

"Each of us," said Plant, "decided to go away and choose a metaphysical type of symbol [that] somehow represented each of us individually—be it a state of mind, an opinion, or something we felt strongly about, or whatever. Then we were to come back together and present our symbols."

"At first I wanted just one symbol," said Page. "But since it was our fourth album and there were four of us, we each chose our own. I designed mine, and everybody else had their own reasons for using the symbol selected."

The four symbols were arranged in a typical magical formation, with the two strongest symbols—

Page's and Plant's, naturally—on the outside, supposedly to protect the weaker two on the inside.

Page's symbol seems to read "ZoSo," though he never intended it to resemble a word. "That's not the pronunciation, it's just a doodle," he claimed. "Although it looks more like writing than the other three, that wasn't the intention." Note, however, that "Zos" was the magical name adopted by artist/magus Austin Osman Spare, a man whose satanic preoccupations rivaled even those of Page's main man Aleister Crowley.

"To this day, I don't know what Jimmy's sign meant," says Richard Cole. "For all I know, he could have been having a fucking laugh with everyone. It could have just been some old [crap] he thought up to get people at it—which is not unlikely with him."

Plant's rune—a feather in a circle—came from Native American symbolism. "My choice involved the feather—a symbol on which all philosophies have been based," Plant explained. "For instance, it represents courage to many Indian tribes. I like people to lay down the truth. No bullshit. That's what it was all about."

Jones's glyph, from Koch's book, was a circle overlaid with three interlocking almond shapes. "John Paul chose his because apparently it needed some precision and dexterity to draw it," Jimmy Page said. Koch himself claimed it was used to ward off evil.

As for Bonzo's three overlapping rings, they represented his feelings about the family life that meant so much to him. "I suppose it's the trilogy—man, woman, and child," Plant remarked. "I suspect it had something to do with the mainstay of all people's belief. At one point, though—in Pittsburgh, I think— we observed that it was also the emblem for Ballantine beer."

The relationship between the runes and the album's cover image is hard to determine. A framed photograph of an old bowler-hatted peasant, stooping beneath the weight of a bundle of branches, hangs on a wall whose flowery paper is peeling badly. When the gatefold sleeve is opened up, we see that the wall belongs to a demolished terrace house, behind which rises a soulless tower block, seen against a glum, off-white sky. (The depressing cityscape was located in Eve Hill, in the Midlands town of Dudley—an area all too familiar to Plant and Bonham. Ironically, the tower block was itself later demolished.)

To the left of the tower block, we can just make out a poster on the wall of a house that's still standing. The band had hoped it would be clearly identifiable as a poster for the Oxfam charity. "Unfortunately, the negatives were a bit of a bluff, so you can't quite read [it]," Page said. "It's the poster where someone is lying dead on a stretcher, and it says that every day somebody receives relief from hunger. You can just make it out on the jacket if you're familiar with the poster."

The sleeve concept for ꙮ⚭⚭⚬ was the joint

creation of Page and Plant—the latter had bought the print of the old man from a junk shop in Reading. "The picture of the old man was Robert's," says Richard Cole. "None of us could work out why the fuck he wanted that old bit of rubbish on the cover." For Page, the picture represented "the old way on a demolished building, with the new way coming up behind it."

As uncomfortable as he looked, in Page's eyes the old man was in harmony with nature. "He takes from nature and gives back to the land," said the guitarist. "It's a natural circle. It's right. His old cottage gets pulled down and they put him in these urban slums, terrible places."

Page-watchers have identified the old man as George Pickingill, a 19th-century witch and sex magician with Masonic and Rosicrucian connections, and a man said to have staged nocturnal orgies in graveyards. (Aleister Crowley is rumored to have been a member of one of Pickingill's covens sometime around 1899.) But the resemblance to "Old George" is unlikely to be more than coincidence. Certainly, Pickingill would have held little appeal for Plant, let alone for Jones and Bonham. "I've never shared those preoccupations with [Jimmy]," Plant said in 2005, "and I don't really know anything about it."

"No one really delved into what Jimmy did, to be honest with you," says Richard Cole. "He didn't really speak about it much. It was as much of a mystery to us as it was to everyone else." (The first that the others knew of the infamous Crowley dictum "Do what thou wilt shall be the whole of the law" that Page had inscribed in the runoff matrix—the spiraling groove that caused the needle to lift off a vinyl LP and return to its dock—of *Led Zeppelin III* was when they first saw the album's test pressing.)

On the inside cover of the gatefold was an illustration—in pencil and gold paint—by artist Barrington Colby, an acquaintance of Page's. Entitled "View in Half or Varying Light," it showed an old, becloaked man standing atop a mountain with a lantern. "The illustration was my idea," said Page. "Some people say it has allusions to [Victorian painter] Henry Holman Hunt, but it hasn't. It actually comes from the idea from the Tarot card of the Hermit, and so the ascension to the beacon and the light of truth. The whole light, so to speak." (Needless to say, there are many who insist the Colby illustration has a more malign occult significance, claiming that when you hold the image up to a mirror, the face of a horned beast is revealed halfway down the mountain. There is also something undeniably sinister about the recreation of Colby's picture in Page's fantasy sequence in *The Song Remains the Same*, filmed near Boleskine House on December 10 and 11, 1973.)

It was Page, too, who chose the art nouveau typeface for the lyrics to "Stairway to Heaven" that were reproduced on the album's inner sleeve. "I found it in a really old arts-and-crafts magazine called *Studio*, which started in the late 1800s," said the part-time aesthete. "I thought the lettering was so interesting, I got someone to work up a whole alphabet."

Hermits and art nouveau typefaces were one thing, but when Atlantic Records got wind of Led Zeppelin's plans to release the album without a title, Ahmet Ertegun and his chief lieutenant Jerry Greenberg had kittens. Page and Peter Grant stood firm, however.

"We had trouble initially, but Ahmet believed in us," Grant recalled. "Again it was a case of following our instincts and knowing that the cover would not harm sales one bit. And we were right again."

"I remember being in an Atlantic office for two hours with a lawyer who was saying, 'You've got to have this,'" Page recalled of a heated meeting in New York. "So I said, 'Alright, run it on the inside bag. Print your Rockefeller Plaza or whatever it is down there.' Of course, they didn't want to have a rerun on it, so there it is. It was a hard job, but fortunately, we were in a position to say, 'This is what we want,' because we had attained the status whereby that album was going to sell a lot."

Robert Plant put it more tersely: "We just said they couldn't have the master tapes until they got the cover right." When Zeppelin played Madison Square Garden on September 3, the singer apologized for the delay in the album's release, adding that "we've got problems trying to get a record cover that looks how we want it." Looking back in the late '80s on the tussle with Atlantic, Plant told Joe Smith that it was "quite hilarious that we followed everything meticulously right down the line."

Atlantic finally backed down, and Led Zeppelin had the album the way they wanted it. When at last it appeared—released on November 8, 1971, in the United States and November 19 in the United Kingdom—it was almost a year since the band had begun work on it.

"Once the album was completed and mixed, I knew it was really good," Page later said. "We actually went on the road in America before the manufacturing process was completed, and somebody at Atlantic said, 'This is professional suicide for a band to tour without an album.' In retrospect, that's rather amusing."

The strain had taken a heavy toll on Led Zeppelin. Touring throughout the year with no new album to promote despite the frequent live airing of its songs, the group had experienced some hairy moments on its travels. On July 5, the group was inadvertently involved in a full-scale riot in the Vigorelli stadium in Milan. Overreacting to the enthusiastic audience of 15,000, police stormed the stadium with tear gas and water cannons.

"When we went in, we could see these riot police," Page remembered. "We saw a few of them in a van, but as we started to play . . . we could see movement [around] the catwalk, and all these riot police coming in. We just carried on playing, and there was smoke at the far end of the outdoor arena, and the promoters ran onstage and said would we tell them to stop lighting fires. So Robert asked them, we carried on playing, and there was a bit more smoke, and suddenly there was smoke by the front of the stage, and it was tear gas!"

After two shows at the Montreux Casino in Switzerland, Zeppelin headed back to North America, beginning a monthlong tour at Vancouver's Pacific Coliseum on August 19. John Bonham later informed Chris Welch that he'd been nervous prior to the tour because he wasn't sure he would still play well. "Stairway" and "California" featured regularly in the set, "Black Dog" and "Rock and Roll"—still being introduced by Plant as "It's Been a Long Time"—only intermittently.

The last dates Led Zeppelin played before the release of ⬧⬧⬧⬧ were five shows in Japan—their first appearances in the Far East. "It was a fantastic place to play," Richard Cole remembered. "The people were so friendly and we had the best promoters looking after us."

"I'm going to do my best to make this the best time we've ever had," Robert Plant announced at the start of the band's first night at Tokyo's legendary Budokan Hall on September 23. "[Because] it seems to be such a difference to America. America doesn't seem to be so good anymore, unfortunately. Maybe it'll get better." Four days later, fittingly, Zeppelin played a benefit concert for victims of the Hiroshima atom bomb.

A much-needed 6-week break preceded the US release of ⚡🜚⚜🜨① and the start of a 16-date UK tour. "Today's the day of the Teddy Bear's picnic," Plant announced from the stage of Newcastle's City Hall on November 11. "And to go with it, the new album came out. I know what they say about the length of time between the two, and I'm sure you can read all sorts of reports and toss a coin!"

Onstage, the four runes could be seen—Page's "ZoSo" displayed on a Marshall speaker cabinet, Bonham's linked circles on his Ludwig bass drum, Jones's symbol draped over his Fender Rhodes electric piano. Less visible, Plant's feather was painted onto a side speaker cabinet. For some of the UK shows, Page wore a "ZoSo" jumper that a fan had specially knitted for him.

On the freezing weekend of November 20 and 21, Zeppelin played two sold-out dates at Wembley's Empire Pool, billed as "Electric Magic" and staged as 5-hour shows that were part circus, part vaudeville, complete with jugglers, acrobats, and even animals. "I expected a bit more from the pigs," Plant remarked, adding that he could have brought some of his own goats along. "This was no job, this was no 'gig,'" wrote *Melody Maker*'s Roy Hollingworth. "It was an event for all."

Despite its stupendous sales over the subsequent decades, ⚡🜚⚜🜨① never actually topped the US album chart. The album was held off the No. 1 spot by—of all things—Carole King's classic *Tapestry*, instead sitting at No. 2 for 5 weeks. (In the United Kingdom, it hit No. 1 on December 4, only to be ousted 2 weeks later by T. Rex's *Electric Warrior*.) But by May 1975, the album had been a permanent resident of the US Top 60 for 3½ years.

In the music press, ⚡🜊⚙◐ met with much of the antipathy that Zeppelin was already accustomed to. "I know that there were originally quite a few people who picked up on the fourth album and gave it a good write-up," commented Page. "But there were the usuals who gave it a good slamming. In England was where we got a major slamming." *Sounds* called ⚡🜊⚙◐ "a much overrated album," with "Black Dog" clattering along "with all the grace and finesse of a farmyard chicken" and "Stairway to Heaven" "inducing first boredom and then catatonia."

But in *Rolling Stone*, future Patti Smith sideman Lenny Kaye was effusive in his praise, describing ⚡🜊⚙◐ as "an album remarkable for its low-keyed and tasteful subtlety" and lauding "the sheer variety of the album," "the incredibly sharp and precise vocal dynamism of Robert Plant," and "some of the tightest arranging and producing Jimmy Page has yet seen his way toward doing."

Even in England there were plaudits. "If *Led Zeppelin III* gave the first indications that their music was by no means confined to power rock," said *Disc*, "then this new album consolidates their expanding maturity. The eight cuts contained herein follow through with unbridled confidence expounding in greater detail the ideas formulated on the previous collection."

Responses such as these went some way to placating the band, who felt that critics had finally stopped prejudging them. "After this record," noted John Paul Jones, "no one ever compared us to Black Sabbath."

"My personal view is that it's the best thing we've ever done," John Bonham told *Melody Maker*'s Chris Welch. "It's the next stage we were at, at the time of recording. The playing is some of the best we've done, and Jimmy is like . . . mint!"

With ⟁⟁⟁⟁ high in the charts on both sides of the Atlantic—and elsewhere around the world— Led Zeppelin was finally able to take time off, reconvening in February 1972 for a tour of Australia and New Zealand.

Jimmy Page had sold the Pangbourne boathouse after flooding had threatened the safety of his equipment, swapping it for a moated Sussex estate called Plumpton Place. In a new home studio he had built at Plumpton, he demo'd riffs for the next Zeppelin album. By late April, the band was working on *Houses of the Holy*.

7

SATANIC MAJESTY

LED ZEPPELIN'S fourth album was not an overnight phenomenon. Though it sold in huge numbers and quickly outstripped the sales of its predecessor, it was only in 1973, when the band undertook their biggest American tour yet—a 3-month slog grossing more than $4 million—that ⚡☯△⊕① began to assume its *Thriller*esque proportions. Much of that had to do with the ever-increasing popularity of "Stairway to Heaven," the cult of which had turned the track into a mystical epic beloved of suburban metalheads from sea to shining sea.

By then Led Zeppelin had recorded and released their fifth album, the somewhat underwhelming *Houses of the Holy*, this time coughing up the cash required for the creature comforts of Mick Jagger's country pile. The fact that *Houses*—classics such as "No Quarter," "The Ocean," and "Over the Hills and Far Away" notwithstanding—was Zeppelin's

Goat's Head Soup (complete with the cod-funk of "The Crunge" and cod-reggae of "D'yer Maker") only made ⚡🜨⚙① sound better.

Whatever Zeppelin themselves felt about *Houses of the Holy*, the morale within the band was as strong as ever. Far from jaded, the quartet was enjoying every minute of its success. "In this band, we're very lucky that everybody is more enthusiastic as time goes on," Robert Plant told *NME*'s Charles Shaar Murray in Los Angeles in June. "There is no fatigue or boredom musically at all."

The singer was even more emphatic in a *Circus* interview 4 months later with Cameron Crowe. "The magnetism that the group holds can't wane for any reason that I can see," Plant said. "We've tried to stay away from all the passing hypes and fads in the musical business. There's no reason why we should follow them at all. We can just set our own standards. I think that people appreciate that. Obviously, I can't see what I'll be doing in 8 years from now . . . but I'll tell you one thing. As long as I'm feeling 'Black Dog,' I'll be singing it."

Crucial to Led Zeppelin's ongoing musical health was the balance within the band—and specifically the chemistry between Plant and Page. ("Pagey and I are closer than ever on this tour," Plant said in 1975. "We've almost jelled into one person in a lot of ways.") Plant's respect for Page's genius was hugely important for the group's internal politics.

"By the time we got to *Houses of the Holy,* and in fact *Physical Graffiti,* all the way down, there was a conscientious air about Jimmy's work," Plant told Steven Rosen in 1983. "And Jimmy's catalytic efforts to get everybody moving one way or the other. It's remarkable that we kept it going for as many records as we did. Really, there wasn't one record that had anything to do with the one before it. And that's a great credit when there are so many artists who will unconsciously rest on their laurels and say, 'This is it, this is the way it must be.'"

Having watched so many bands unravel acrimoniously over the years, Page himself was proud of Led Zeppelin's staying power. "The group has been going for a long time now," he told Mick Houghton in 1976. "There are too many groups that have broken up or changed personnel for whatever reason, and it's so unfortunate. Whenever we sit down and talk about the future, there's always this bond that we're gonna go on forever. There's no splinter thing like solo albums. If there ever were solo albums, it wouldn't be because somebody was so frustrated that he couldn't get what he wanted out within the group unit. The creative process may change, you never know, but we're confident it will stay as it is."

"They were fantastic," Peter Grant reflected in 1993. "Part of the success was that we never hung out at the Speakeasy or wherever. We got together when we needed to and then did our own thing. That's why I always tried to make sure we didn't overdo the touring during the school holidays, so the guys could see their children. We didn't live in each other's pockets."

"We're not too close, not so that every little thing bothers us," John Bonham said. "If one of us is ill, the rest of us don't all come out in rashes too. We're close in another way."

The solidarity within Led Zeppelin was perhaps all the more surprising when one considers the tales of decadence and debauchery that followed the group around the world. After ⚡ made them the biggest band on earth, their status as Learjet libertines almost came to overshadow their music. To this day, Led Zeppelin remains a byword for rock excess, macho affluence on a swollen scale. As Erik Davis wrote, "the enjoyment that Led Zeppelin has given so many of us is partly a function of our fantasies about their own engorged enjoyment of the world."

"The rule book hadn't been written yet," Robert Plant later remarked. "We were the standard-bearers, from which that patent has been used so many times now."

"The Beatles kind of opened the door to it," said Henry Smith, "but the Beatles never did it the way rock and roll did it. When the Who came over and Zeppelin was there, they were the bad boys of rock and roll. Now, whether or not Peter used that as a tool—and in some ways I think he probably did—there's nothing like a bad reputation to take you a long way. The Stones went places because the Beatles were the good boys and the Stones were the bad boys. And Zeppelin was the bad boys too. I think some of that mystique helped them in that time period."

Hooligan aesthetes running riot in the corridors of America's best hotels, Zeppelin flew the flag for British hedonism, "basking"—in the words of Lenny Kaye and David Dalton—"in the glory of stardom." ("Next time you need two motorcycles and a live octopus at 3:00 in the morning," a Zeppelin roadie grouched good-humoredly at Plant on the 1973 US tour, "go ask someone else!") And nowhere was this more apparent than in Los Angeles.

"LA had a mystique," Henry Smith continues. "It's warm, and when you get in the warmth, you kind of let your hair down. Whenever we went there, it was a hub, it was the place to be. Drugs were easy to get, so when we arrived it was like, 'Okay, we've finished the gloomy part of the US, which is anything between Cleveland and Denver, and where there's nothing to do.'"

Life at LA's Continental Hyatt House (or "Riot House") involved cricket matches and motorcycle races in the hallway, along with the inevitable chairs and TV sets being flung from windows. In the UK tabloid *The Sun*, reporter Bob Hart wrote of "an English girl who was the coke lady . . . so nobody else ever carried or touched coke. . . ." He also noted "the terrible treatment of girls" by the Zeppelin camp.

"Now I would look back on it with kind of a giggle," said Henry Smith. "But in those days, I suppose I would have looked at it, going, 'How dare they come over here and treat our women that way?' Did we cross the line sometimes? Oh yeah. We were lucky we didn't get arrested—for all sorts of things."

"The downfall of the '60s dream was very disappointing, because we'd really thought we could change things," said Pamela Des Barres, who saw the band's antics in Hollywood Babylon up close. "As much as I loved Zeppelin, they kind of fucked things up in LA. Something about their energy really altered the *joie de vivre* of the scene. They thought they could get away with anything, and they could, because everybody wanted to get near them. They were very debauched, and the girls got younger and more willing to do anything. It got to be incredibly sick."

The former Miss Pamela had personal reasons for chiding the band, having been jilted as Jimmy Page's LA squeeze in favor of pubescent über-groupie Lori Lightning (nee Lori Maddox). "There was such backstabbing in the groupie scene," she said. "In the '60s, we were all *for* each other—there was a feeling that was more important than any one *guy*."

"The original groupies were a lot quieter and lower-key," said Richard Cole. "With the second-generation girls in LA, there was more hysteria there, because they were trying to live up to what they'd read or heard about without really knowing how to do it. Girls like Pamela weren't really groupies in comparison to what came later. They were a great bunch of girls, and we had a hell of a lot of fun with them, but they weren't throwing the sex on the table. Sometimes there was sex involved, sometimes there wasn't."

"The really famous groupies were extremely tough and unpleasant," concured Nick Kent, the *NME* journalist who wrote regularly about Zeppelin in the '70s. "Jimmy told me that one of his Hollywood girlfriends bit into a sandwich that had razor blades in it. Seeing these conniving, loveless little girls really affected my concept of femininity for a while."

Kent claims that in all his years as a rock writer, he never saw anybody behave worse than John Bonham or Richard Cole. "I once saw them beat a guy senseless for no reason and then drop money on his face," Kent said. "It makes me feel sick when I hear Plant talking about what a great geezer Bonzo was, because the guy was a schizophrenic animal. He was like something out of *Straw Dogs*."

"Well, Nick Kent was a groupie," Plant countered. "He was with Keith [Richards] or he was with Jimmy. And the psyche of that condition and that platform from where he made his assertions was based on the chemicals and the humor. Nick went where he felt the greatest affinity, comfort, and stimulation, so to look at Bonzo coming in growling, with a suit and a fedora on and carrying a black stick with a silver top . . . see, the social intrigue of a group of people on the road was such that people who were with me wanted to know what on earth was going on in another area."

Cole wasn't much better, amiable bloke though he's become. "It's weird to see Richard today," said Pamela Des Barres, "because I have images of him kicking people's teeth out."

"We didn't give a fuck," Cole said. "The doors had to open now. If they didn't, we'd break them down. And that was it. We made our own laws. If you didn't want to fucking abide by them, don't get involved."

"They were like a bunch of footballers, crude and rude," recalled Peter Clifton, a director brought in to help salvage Zeppelin's glorified "home movie" *The Song Remains the Same.* "In fact, they took a real pleasure in being rude to people." *Melody Maker*'s Chris Charlesworth, an ally of the band, admitted that "it was very intimidating to be around Led Zeppelin in those days."

To this day, however, the surviving members of the band feel their hell-raising reputation has been overplayed. Much of that is due to Stephen Davis's sensationalist *Hammer of the Gods*, a book based heavily on Cole's reminiscences.

"I want to believe *Hammer of the Gods* because it's done us huge favors in terms of aura," Robert Plant told *Mojo*'s Mat Snow in 1994. "I once saw Kenny Hibbitt [a soccer hero of Plant's in the '70s] pissed on a Friday night. I was furious. I went home and I couldn't sleep. Terrible."

"The debauchery was more people like Richard and me than it was the band," admitted Henry Smith. "The band just got the credit for it."

In Davis's book, Cole himself confessed that "all the so-called Led Zeppelin depravity took place the first 2 years in an alcoholic fog." "I don't think it was an attitude, really," he says today, "except that we were perhaps a little more extravagant. It's like someone going on holiday. I mean, you're not going to do at home what you do on holiday—misbehaving and getting blind drunk and getting up to all sorts of tricks."

By 1972, Cole claimed, "we got older and grew out of it," adding that Led Zeppelin "became a realistic business." In 1975, Robert Plant said the band was "more into staying in our rooms and reading Nietzsche," though possibly he wasn't speaking for John Bonham.

"Flying with them, it was surprising how quiet and well-behaved it all was," recalled Chris Welch, who often accompanied Zeppelin on tour as a *Melody Maker* reporter. "They weren't rioting all the time on a continental hotel-wrecking spree. Robert would be reading *Country Life*, choosing his next country mansion, and Jimmy would spend his free time in each city buying antiques."

"I like to think people know that we're pretty raunchy and that we really do a lot of the things people say we do," Plant told Lisa Robinson in May 1973. "But what we're getting across [onstage] is goodness.

It ain't 'Stand up and put your fist in the air—we want revolution.'"

Plant was no innocent, though. Years later, Robinson wrote that his "tour amours" were "girls he managed to convince that he was, at any given moment, about to leave his wife, Maureen. . . ." She recounted the story that Maureen once came running out of the farmhouse with a copy of *Melody Maker* featuring a picture of Zeppelin surrounded by the jailbait at Rodney Bingenheimer's English Disco club. "Maureen!" Plant is said to have responded, "you *know* we don't take the *Maker*!"

It didn't help that 1973 also saw the publication of *Trips*, by another female rock journalist, Ellen Sander. In the book, Sander alleged that she'd almost been gang-raped by two members of Led Zeppelin in 1969. "If you walk inside the cages of the zoo," she wrote, "you get to see the animals close up, stroke the captive pelts and mingle with the energy behind the mystique. You also get to smell the shit first hand."

"I'm probably more ashamed of the *reputation* than of anything we actually did," said John Paul Jones, the Bill Wyman of Led Zeppelin, and a man who claimed that "nothing exciting" ever happened to him. "Plus it seems to me they've forgotten every other band that was there, and it seemed to me that everybody was behaving in a similar way. People have put this really evil slant on it, but it was really more just high spirits. I read these things and think, 'Are they really talking about *us*?' I mean, we used to follow the Who places and they were still *redecorating* after them. We took the heat for everybody. With LA, the problem was it was so *boring* most of the time that as soon as any life arrived, suddenly you ruled the town!"

It was particularly irksome to Zeppelin that the Rolling Stones was as fawned over by the media as Zeppelin were vilified by them. (Unlike the Stones—and despite the patronage of Ahmet Ertegun—Zeppelin was never part of the chic New York circle surrounding Andy Warhol. They were never accompanied on tour by Truman Capote and Princess Lee Radziwill.) "We knew full well that we were doing more business than them," Plant told Crowe. "We were getting better gates in comparison to a lot of people who were constantly glorified in the press."

After Zeppelin's 1972 tour of America, Peter Grant decided to take action, hiring publicist B. P. Fallon to bring the band kudos and credibility. "Without getting too egocentric," Plant told Cameron Crowe, "we thought it was time that people heard something about us other than that we were eating women and throwing the bones out the window."

The band members themselves were increasingly torn between their two lives: the madness of the road, the restorative calm of home. As Stephen Davis wrote in *Hammer of the Gods*, "Led Zeppelin lived in two worlds, one a secure green England of family and tradition, the other a lurid Hollywood movie of fantasy and excess."

No one exemplified this better than John Bonham, whose behavior on tour was at least partly a response to the homesickness and anxiety he felt at being separated from his wife and children. "[Bonzo] was a loving, responsible parent," Robert Plant told Mick Wall. "And underneath all the brash bravado . . . he was very reliant on [his wife]. They fought like cats and dogs, but they loved each other tremendously." This is the family man we see in *The Song Remains the Same*: Bonzo on his tractor, Bonzo with his cows, Bonzo with Pat Bonham and young Jason on a drum kit.

"Bonzo drank because he hated being away from home, he really did," said John Paul Jones. "Between gigs, he found it hard to cope. And he hated flying. Sometimes he'd drink before getting on a plane and ask the driver to turn round and take him home."

"Bonzo was much more meat-and-potatoes than, say, Robert," said Richard Cole. "It was always, 'I don't like all this foreign food.' And when you went to his house in the south of France when they were tax exiles, the pantry was like the corner shop—Bird's custard [a cornflour-based custard], you name it, it was in there." Killing time during a technical problem at the LA Forum on June 21, 1977, Plant described Bonham as— among other things—"the man who said he could go back to a building site anytime . . . and we all agreed."

A surlier, more *lumpen* version of Keith Moon,

Bonham was becoming a liability for Led Zeppelin. Had they not had endless cash to throw at the problem, the drummer's career might have come to an unsavory end a lot earlier than it did. "He was a big overgrown baby," recalled Linda Alderetti, a cashier at LA's Rainbow Bar & Grill who became a regular companion of the drummer's. "He did not grow up with much sophistication, and he was not very bright."

Certainly not as bright as Robert Plant, himself torn in two by Zeppelin's double life. "There's constant conflict, really, within me," the singer told Cameron Crowe in a big interview that was partly an opportunity for *Rolling Stone* to atone for their treatment of the band. "As much as I really enjoy what I do at home . . . I play on my own little soccer team and I've been taking part in the community and living the life of any ordinary guy. I always find myself wistful and enveloped in a feeling I can't really get out of my system. I miss this band when we aren't playing."

Plant, still a hippie at heart, would have agreed with Pamela Des Barres's assessment that the LA scene had become tarnished beyond recognition. "LA was LA," he told Crowe. "It's not LA now. LA infested with jaded 12-year-olds is not the LA that I really dug. I haven't lost my innocence particularly. I'm always ready to pretend I haven't. Yeah, it is a shame in a way. And it's a shame to see these young chicks bungle their lives away in a flurry and rush to compete with what was in the old days, the good-time relationships we had with the GTOs and people like that. When it came to looning, they could give us as much of a looning as we could give them."

Plant addressed the subject on *Physical Graffiti*'s "Sick Again," a song about LA's platform-booted Lolitas. "*Clutching pages from your teenage dream in the lobby of the Hotel Paradise,*" he sang; "*through the circus of the LA queens, how fast you learn the downhill slide.*"

"The words show I feel a bit sorry for them," he told Cameron Crowe. "One minute she's 12 and the next minute she's 13 and over the top. Such a shame. They haven't got the style that they had in the old days . . . way back in '68."

LA groupies aside, Zeppelin's US tours became increasingly debilitating for the band. Plant damaged his voice so badly during the summer of 1973 that he was forced to undergo an operation on his vocal cords before the group could resume work on *Physical Graffiti* in early 1974. The filming of *The Song Remains the Same*—which included live footage from the group's Madison Square Garden shows in July—didn't help matters. At one point, John Paul Jones informed Peter Grant that he'd had enough and wanted to quit.

"It was kept low-key," Grant remembered. "I told Jimmy, of course, who couldn't believe it. But it was the pressure. He was a family man, was Jonesy. Eventually, I think he realized he was doing something he really loved. It was never discussed again."

As for Jimmy Page, corruptor of Lori Lightning and other nubile ultravixens, the US tour of 1973 left him completely burned out. "I was thinking that I should be in either a mental hospital or a monastery," he recalled. "It was like the adrenaline tap wouldn't switch off. . . ." The guitarist's use of cocaine can only have exacerbated that sensation.

To Cameron Crowe, Page emphasized that he loved playing live as much as he'd ever done. "If it was down to just that, it would be utopia," he said. "But it's not. It's airplanes, hotel rooms, limousines, and armed guards standing outside rooms. I don't get off on that part of it all." (He added that he was "still searching for an angel with a broken wing," adding that it wasn't "easy to find them these days, especially when you're staying at the Plaza Hotel.")

Physically shattered, Page nonetheless symbolized Led Zeppelin's satanic majesty. The guitarist's enervated appearance and sphinx-like smile suggested some malign force lurked beneath the surface. "This was not a wholesome man," wrote Erik Davis after cataloging "the silk threads emblazoned with poppies and magus stars, the SS cap, [and] the slit puffy eyelids that lent his face a stoned Orientalism." The ongoing stories about Jimmy's obsession with Aleister Crowley only bolstered his sinister reputation.

Known as "the Wickedest Man in the World," Crowley (1875–1947) was a writer, painter, occultist, and sexual libertarian who wrote about and practiced the magic arts in the early 20th century. After breaking with the Hermetic Order of the Golden Dawn, he formed a mystical system known as Thelema, based on the primacy of the individual will. "Do what thou wilt shall be the whole of the law" was one of the principal commandments of his philosophy. His publications included *The Book of the Law* and *Diary of a Drug Fiend*.

"I don't want to do a huge job on Crowley or anything," Page told Nick Kent. "I mean, if people are into reading Crowley, then they will and it'll have nothing to do with me. It's just . . . well, for me, it goes without saying that Crowley was grossly misunderstood . . . I mean, how can anyone call Crowley the world's most evil man—and that carried over to the '30s when Hitler was about?"

Page had been fascinated by the occult and by parapsychology since the age of 11, when he claimed to have first read Crowley's *Magic in Theory and Practice*. In 1975, he opened the Equinox, a Kensington bookshop that sold occult literature and specialized in Crowley's works, even publishing the facsimile of a 16th-century magical text called *The Book of the Goetia of Solomon the King*, edited and originally published by Crowley in 1904.

He told *Sounds*'s Jonh Ingham that Crowley was "a misunderstood genius of the 20th century," adding that "[Crowley's] whole thing was liberation of the person, of the entity, and that restriction would foul you up, lead to frustration [that] leads to violence, crime, mental breakdown, depending on what sort of makeup you have underneath."

Yet as much as he championed Crowley as a force for "liberation," Page loved to revel in the more macabre aspects of his hero's life. Asked about Boleskine House, which Crowley had bought in 1899 with a view to attempting a magical rite known as The Operation of Abra-Melin the Mage, he said that a man had been beheaded there and that "sometimes you can hear his head rolling down." Since Crowley had moved out of Boleskine, Jimmy added, "there have been suicides, people carted off to mental hospitals. . . ."

Plumpton Place, it seems, was almost as spooky as Boleskine. "All my houses are isolated," he told Cameron Crowe. "Many is the time I just stay home alone. I mean, I could tell you things, but it might give people ideas. A few things have happened that would freak some people out, but I was surprised actually at how composed I was."

"Jimmy was incredible," singer Michael Des Barres told Stephen Davis. "Because he was the classic rock star with the moated castle, the velvet clothes, the fabulous cars he couldn't drive, and the 80,000 rare guitars. I was dabbling with the Crowley thing at the time. I used to go down to see Jimmy at Plumpton and he'd pull out Crowley's robes, Crowley's Tarot deck, all of Crowley's gear that he'd collected. I thought, 'This is great.' It was all so twisted and debauched, their whole thing. That's what Jimmy represented to me."

Not long after Page moved to Plumpton, he received another visitor, a man who gave his Crowley fixation a new slant. American avant-garde director Kenneth Anger was at work on a Crowley-inspired film called *Lucifer Rising*, and he had become aware of the guitarist's interest in "The Great Beast" when outbid by him in an auction for a rare Crowley manuscript at Sotheby's. Anger, who had himself spent time at Boleskine, came to Sussex to ask whether Page would be interested in composing the soundtrack for his film.

Page, who admired Anger's earlier film *Invocation of My Demon Brother*, was intrigued by the proposal and accepted the director's offer. He quickly decided that the music would all be played on synthesizers.

"With a synthesizer, every instrument is different from what it's meant to sound like," Page told Nick Kent. "Which is especially interesting when you get a collage of instruments together not sounding the way they should and you think, 'What's that?' That's the effect I wanted to get, so you didn't immediately realize it was five instruments playing together. Because Anger's visuals have a timeless aspect."

Page was so entranced by the 20-minute clip of *Lucifer Rising* that Anger had given him that he would endlessly play it in hotel rooms, sometimes to friends such as David Bowie and usually under the influence of cocaine.

"It's just so arresting," he said. "I had a copy, and while I was in the States, I hooked it up to a big stereo and frightened the daylights out of everyone. I was on the sixth floor and there were complaints from the twelfth. There's a real atmosphere and intensity. It's disturbing because you know something's coming. I can't wait for it to come out."

The relationship with Anger, however, was destined to be an unhappy one. Page remained smitten with Anger's cinematic style, but the director became increasingly impatient with the guitarist's laissez-faire attitude and drugged-out procrastination.

By 1977, things had reached the boiling point. For several months, Anger used film-editing equipment in the basement of Page's London home, but one night in the fall of that year, he was abruptly banished from the house.

"I haven't laid eyes on Jimmy Page since early June," the director said after rescuing his film from the house. "I've been trying to get in contact with him since then. I've fixed meetings through his office and been stood up half a dozen times. I've left messages on his Kafkaesque answering machine. All I've had is promises that the soundtrack is on its way, but nothing's materialized. I've got a fucking film to finish."

Anger said that Page's behavior was "totally contradictory to the teachings of Aleister Crowley and totally contradictory to the ethos of the film," adding that Page was "dried up as a musician" and didn't have another "Stairway to Heaven" in him. "I'm seriously questioning whether to use a musician from the rock world," he said. "It seems like most of today's rock music is savage, deliberate bad taste. It's not optimistic, constructive, or even fun anymore." Page's replacement? Charles Manson acolyte Bobby Beausoleil.

Asked about the hostility between him and Anger, Page tried to be diplomatic. "I think it's more the problems he's had with himself," he told Chris Salewicz. "All I know is that at the end of the film, I promised him—as I had before—the loan of a three-speed projector, which makes the editing so much easier. I said to him, 'Well, it's just going to be your own time invested.' And I also told him that he must put the music on after he put the footage together, so I was just waiting for him to contact me, really. He had other music that I'd done instead of the stuff that I'd delivered, which he said he wanted to use. Nevertheless, I still needed to hear from him. And I never heard anything."

Matters reached a diabolical crescendo when Anger nailed a black-magic curse to the doors of Led Zeppelin's record company, Swan Song. "It was pathetic," Page said. "His curse amounted to sending letters to people. Silly letters saying 'Bugger off, Page' and this sort of thing."

Anger had the last word, however. "I'm certainly jaded with the rock superstar syndrome," he said of his dealings with Page. "They're like renaissance bandits. Who needs those people?"

8

WHAT IS AND WHAT SHOULD NEVER BE

1975 WAS the year of *Physical Graffiti*—the last testament of Led Zeppelin at Headley Grange—and of the band's legendary 5-night stand at London's Earl's Court arena. But it was also the year in which Robert and Maureen Plant nearly died after their hired car careered off a mountain road on the Greek island of Rhodes.

"I know that my kind of vision, or the carefree element I had, disappeared instantly when I had my accident," Plant told Joe Smith. "That kind of ramshackle 'I'll take the world now' attitude was completely gone."

Plant was still in a wheelchair when Zeppelin recorded *Presence* at Munich's Musicland studios in November of that year. If the sessions lifted the singer's spirits, the music was tired and labored.

"Achilles' Last Stand" was a thunderous 10-minute epic, and "Tea for One" harked back to the scorched blues balladry of "Since I've Been Loving You." But on most of *Presence*, inspiration was notable by its absence. On the eve of punk, the album was nothing short of dull, and Led Zeppelin had never been dull.

Much of 1976 was spent on sabbatical, with Plant slowly recuperating from the accident while the band worked on the finishing stages of *The Song Remains the Same*. 1977 saw them return to America with a vengeance, setting a new indoor-arena record when more than 76,000 saw them at the Pontiac Silverdome in Michigan on April 30. The band also repeated its weeklong Earl's Court stand with 6-night residencies at Madison Square Garden and the LA Forum.

"It's funny," said John Paul Jones. "After playing to 70,000 people, going back to Madison Square Garden was like a small club again. It was like, 'Ah, this is cozy!'"

Not so cozy was the violent altercation that occurred backstage at Oakland's Alameda County Coliseum on July 23 when Peter Grant, Richard Cole, and Zeppelin heavy John Bindon beat up three members of promoter Bill Graham's security staff.

The US tour was almost over when Robert Plant was hit with the devastating news that a severe respiratory virus had killed his 6-year-old son, Karac, in England. The band did not play live again for another

2 years. During that period, moreover, Zeppelin's collective health declined drastically.

"It was just a mess," remembers Robert Plant, who sank into deep grief and depression, barely able to see the point of music. "After the death of my son, I received a lot of support from Bonzo, and I went through the mill because the media turned on the whole thing and made it even worse. I found that the excesses that surrounded Led Zeppelin were such that nobody knew where the actual axis of all this stuff was. Everybody was insular, developing their own world. The band had gone through two or three really big—*huge*—changes. The whole beauty and lightness of 1970 had turned into a sort of neurosis."

Plant healed at home, tending to his family and withdrawing to the local pub. "I tinkered on the village piano," he said, "and grew so obese drinking beer that nobody knew who I was." When the worst of the grief was past, he applied to take a job at a Rudolph Steiner teacher's college in Sussex.

With Jimmy Page scrambling to deny that the group was calling it a day—and to refute the callous insinuations that his Crowley fixation was somehow to blame for Karac's death—Zeppelin attempted to get themselves back on track with a meeting in May 1978 at Clearwell Castle in the Forest of Dean. It was Bonham who persuaded his old Birmingham friend to join them.

"Bonzo came over and worked on me a few times with the aid of a bottle of gin," Plant remembered.

"He was the only guy that actually hugged me, that helped me at all. And he said, 'C'mon, we're gonna go down to Clearwell and try some writing.' But it had changed so much. And I really like being light and being happy, and it was just almost turning up to keep it going in a way."

"I think Robert was interested," said John Paul Jones, "but he was seeing things in a different light. He was wondering whether it was all worth it. He and I were getting a bit closer, and probably splitting from the other two in a way. We were always to be found over a pint somewhere thinking, 'What are we *doing*?'"

It didn't help that Page and Bonham were in the grip of drink and drugs—heroin included—in ways that Plant and Jones had never been. "These days everybody knows so much about helping people, but in those days it was other people's personal life and area," Jones said. "And while you say, 'For Christ's sake, don't do this' or 'Be here then,' you didn't really know enough to start telling other people how to live their lives. We were beginning, I suppose, to think, 'Well, wait a minute, it may be coming apart more than it should.'"

The growing schism between Plant/Jones and Page/Bonham was only too evident when the group left for Stockholm in late 1978 to record their ninth album.

"The band was splitting between people who could

turn up at recording sessions on time and people who couldn't," said Jones with a serene smile. "I mean, we all got together and made the album in the end, but it wasn't quite as open as it was in the early days." The more nocturnal contributions of the guitarist and the drummer brought the others still closer. Indeed, Plant and Jones wound up writing most of *In Through the Out Door.*

"It was kind of odd," said Plant, "but it gave the whole thing a different feel and a different texture. When Jimmy came in, his contribution generally was spot-on. We weren't gonna make another 'Communication Breakdown,' but I thought 'In the Evening' was really good, and I thought parts of 'Carouselambra' were good, especially the darker dirges that Pagey developed. The lyrics on 'Carouselambra' were actually about that environment and that situation. The whole story of Led Zeppelin in its latter years is in that song."

"Powerless the fabled sat, too smug to lift a hand," Plant sang in one of the song's most telling couplets; *"toward the foe that threatened from the deep."* Jimmy Page, however, is keen to dispel some of the rumors about the threat. "There are people who say, 'Oh, Jimmy wasn't in very good shape,'" he said. "But what I do know is that *Presence* was recorded and mixed in 3 weeks, and *In Through the Out Door* was done in a little over 3 weeks. So I couldn't have been in *that* bad a shape."

In Through the Out Door was pretty poor. The riffs were lame, the choruses limp, the keyboards cheesy. There was no blues groove to any of the seven tracks. The album sounded like a hard rock band trying to reinvent itself as some kind of AOR/new wave hybrid. "Carouselambra" was over-exaggerated progressive rock. The funky-shuffle muso-samba of "Fool in the Rain" was unconvincing and couldn't mask the fact that Plant's singing was flat. The bland boogie of "South Bound Saurez" and the knees-up hoedown of "Hot Dog" were hopeless. Only "All My Love," an elegy for Karac, was affecting on any level whatsoever.

"1979 dawned with the album done," said Plant. "I was lucky enough to be given another son, Logan. It was lifting again. And we decided we could work, and we should start all over again. We'd done these things again, like 'Led Zeppelin Go Back to the Clubs.' Well, [crap]. Playing Nottingham Boat Club for four cases of Nut Brown. All these great ideas in that great naive time. But it was agreed that we should play in England, and the preparations were made for Knebworth."

At the beginning of August 1979, Zeppelin played two shows in front of more than a quarter of a million people at Knebworth, the Hertfordshire estate where five festivals had been held in the '70s. Not having played live in Britain since Earl's Court shows of 1975, the four horsemen were scared to death.

"It was dumbfounding to see what had happened,

that 260,000 tickets had been sold in 2 days," recalled Plant, who'd been reluctant to do the shows. "Fred Bannister, who used to book me in the Town Hall in Stourbridge for 8 quid [or approximately $15 US], was going, 'Well, I say, Robert, I think you've made a bit of a killing here.' And in some ways it was a bit of a shambles, and in another way I think I was a bit embarrassed about how big it was."

"Robert didn't want to do it, and I could understand why," said Jones. "But *we* really did, and we thought he would enjoy it if we could just get him back out there. And I think he *did* enjoy Knebworth. On the DVD he *looks* like he's enjoying it!"

"I watched it on the DVD and thought, 'Christ, that was crap,'" Plant said. "I knew how good we had been, and we were so nervous. And yet within it all, my old pal Bonzo was right down in a pocket. And I'd thought he was speeding up on the night—I must have been so nervous myself that every single blemish and twist that was just a little bit away from what I expected was making me a little bit hyper. But for all that went wrong, if you listen to 'Achilles' Last Stand' from Knebworth, it's absolutely spectacular. It's prog [progressive] rock gone mad."

"The reality of Knebworth was that it was fantastic," said Page. "I mean, we had to come in by helicopter, and you could see this huge sea of people. It was astonishing."

"After it was over," said Plant, "I don't know if I

was breathing a sigh of relief because we'd got to the end of the show in one piece or whether we'd actually bought some more time to keep going."

For all three surviving members, the What Might Have Been factor in Led Zeppelin's story still weighs heavy. "The band had been on its knees," said Plant. "The cause and effect of all that success had taken its toll, and we *just* managed to get back. And just as we started to move again. . . ."

On September 24, 1980, at Jimmy Page's new Thameside mansion near Windsor, John Bonham died after drinking a vast amount of vodka and being helped to a bedroom by Page's assistant Rick Hobbs. The pathologist's report stated that the cause was pulmonary edema: Bonzo had drowned in his own vomit.

"Who knows where we would have gone?" said Page. "Maybe the band would have broken up. I don't know. But what I do know is that Bonzo and I had discussed that the next album was going to be more hard-hitting. I don't know how that would have turned out."

For Plant in particular, Bonham's death meant definitively that Led Zeppelin was no more. Apart from a reunion appearance at Atlantic Records' 40th birthday party at Madison Square Garden in 1988—and despite reuniting with Jimmy Page for the '90s albums *No Quarter* and *Walking into Clarksdale*—the singer has consistently resisted attempts to resurrect the behemoth that the band represented.

"I wanted to establish an identity that was far removed from the howling and the mud sharks of the '70s," he told *Rolling Stone*'s David Fricke in 1988. To Joe Smith in the same period, he said he was "trying to make some kind of move on my own terms, without the hysteria that was common to that great epoch." In 1994, he admitted to *Mojo*'s Mat Snow that he'd "denied Led Zeppelin's existence because I didn't want to end up like a fucking fat mouse in a trap."

"[A Zeppelin reunion] would have been a vast earner and it would have outsold anyone, including the Stones," Peter Grant admitted in 1993. "But would they have been any happier? I know Jimmy was keen, but Robert didn't want to do it. [And] let's face it, it wouldn't be the same. If they had done it, that invaluable Zeppelin mystique would have gone forever."

My peers may flirt with cabaret, some fake the rebel yell," Plant sang on his blistering 2005 track "Tin Pan Valley." "*I'm moving up to higher ground, I must escape their hell.*" That year, Plant declined to appear at the Grammy Awards when Led Zeppelin received a Lifetime Achievement award, prompting Page's pained words, "It wouldn't have taken much to just pop over, would it?"

Yet Plant remains deeply proud of his achievements in Led Zeppelin. "We questioned the whole order of things," he told *Vanity Fair*'s Lisa Robinson in 2003, "and not just for one or two albums for 10 years." He also remains hurt and perplexed at the critical kicking the group received. "How can we be reviled in so many different generations," he asked Robinson rhetorically, "and then find out that we were the people's favorite band?"

"The funny thing about Led Zeppelin," said Jack White, "was that American rock radio just played the shit out of them, to the point where it was almost embarrassing to like them. Because it was *too obvious*. It was almost like quoting *Spinal Tap* in front of other musicians, and it's not funny to say it out loud anymore. It's one of those things where you're more likely to have a statue of Led Zeppelin in your house than to actually mention them in conversation. It kind of represents so much in that realm, because of punk rock destroying [progressive] rock and all the big regular rock."

"My position in the game is so radically different to the way it was then," Robert Plant told me. "What was a priority then has gone; it's completely passed. I don't see Zeppelin as any sort of stigma or impediment for my future, and it would be good to see what could happen. But that means that you reinvoke that tired old harness. And I'm very, very happy where I am musically."

Thirty-five years after their fourth album made Led Zeppelin the biggest, loudest, most demonically powerful band on Earth, their unabashed endorsement by such leading lights of 21st-century rock as the White Stripes is a fitting kind of justice. Twenty-two million copies sold (and counting) has made

ZOSO a yardstick for western rock, an unmatched and unavoidable touchstone that also happens to be the greatest work by the greatest hard rock band of all time.

"From the first rehearsal onward, there was no dead weight in Led Zeppelin," said John Paul Jones. "It was a very strong lineup, and I'm not that modest about it. It wasn't like, 'Oh, the drummer's dad owns the van so we'll have to put up with him.' Listening to Zeppelin now, it only dates because of the recording techniques, like the amount of bass drum there is. The music itself is timeless."

SELECTED BIBLIOGRAPHY

Altham, Keith. "Only Jimmy Left to Form the New Yardbirds." *New Musical Express,* October 1968.

———. "Led Zeppelin Are Not Prefabricated." *Top Pops,* September 1969.

Burroughs, William. "Rock Magic: Jimmy Page, Led Zeppelin, and a Search for the Elusive Stairway to Heaven." *Crawdaddy,* June 1975.

Cole, Richard, with Richard Trubo. *Stairway to Heaven: Led Zeppelin Uncensored.* New York: HarperCollins, 1992.

Crowe, Cameron. "Led Zep Won't Stop Touring." *Circus,* November 1973.

———. "The Durable Led Zeppelin: A Conversation with Jimmy Page and Robert Plant." *Rolling Stone,* March 1975.

———. "Led Zep Conquers States, 'Beast' Prowls to the Din of Hordes." *Rolling Stone,* May 1975.

Davis, Erik. [symbols] (331/3). New York: Continuum International Publishing Group, 2005.

Davis, Stephen. *Hammer of the Gods: Led Zeppelin Unauthorised.* London: Pan, 1995.

Eddy, Chuck. *Stairway to Hell: The 500 Best Heavy Metal Albums in the Universe.* New York: Harmony, 1991.

Fast, Susan. *In the Houses of the Holy: Led Zeppelin and the Power of Rock Music*. New York: Oxford University Press, 2001.

Fricke, David. "Robert Plant: The Rolling Stone Interview." *Rolling Stone*, March 1988.

Fyfe, Andy. *When the Levee Breaks: The Making of Led Zeppelin IV*. London: Unanimous, 2003.

Godwin, Robert. *The Making of Led Zeppelin's* ⚡☯♁☉ Burlington, Ontario: CG Publishing, 1996.

———. *Led Zeppelin: The Press Reports*. Burlington, Ontario: CG Publishing, 2003.

Grundy, Stuart, and John Tobler. *The Guitar Greats*. London: BBC Books, 1983.

Hoskyns, Barney. "Been a Long Time: Led Zeppelin." *Mojo*, July 2003.

———. "Stairway to Snowdonia: Rapping with Robert Plant." Rock's Backpages [www.rocksbackpages.com], October 2003.

Houghton, Mick. "Zeus of Zeppelin: An Interview with Jimmy Page." *Circus*, October 1976.

Ingham, Jonh. "Jimmy Page: Technological Gypsy." *Sounds*, March 1976.

Kaye, Lenny. Review of Led Zeppelin IV. *Rolling Stone*, December 1971.

Lewis, Dave. *Led Zeppelin: The Tight But Loose Files*. London: Omnibus, 2003.

Lewis, Dave, with Simon Pallett. *Led Zeppelin: The Concert File*. London: Omnibus, 2005.

McGrath, Rick. Interview with Led Zeppelin. *The Georgia Straight*, Fall 1971.

Mendelssohn, John. Review of Led Zeppelin II. *Rolling Stone*, December 1969.

Murray, Charles Shaar. "Robert Plant—And That Below-the-Belt Surge." *New Musical Express*, June 1973.

Robinson, Lisa. "Stairway to Excess." *Vanity Fair*, November 2003.

Rosen, Steven. "Steel Driven Led." *Sounds*, June 1973.

———. "Jimmy Page." *Guitar Player*, July 1977.

Ross, Ron. "Zeppelin '75." *Phonograph Record*, March 1975.

Salewicz, Chris. "The Gig Interview: Jimmy Page." *Gig*, May 1977.

Schulps, Dave. "Jimmy Page: The Trouser Press Interview." *Trouser Press*, Fall 1977.

Shade, Will. "Thieving Magpies: Jimmy Page's Dubious Recording Legacy." *Perfect Sound Forever* [www.furious. com/Perfect], January 2001.

Sutcliffe, Phil. "Getting It Together at Bron-Y-Aur: The Story of Led Zeppelin III." *Mojo*, April 2000.

Turner, Steve. "Stairway to Heaven, Paved with Gold: Led Zeppelin's Snowdonia." *The Independent*, April 1991.

Welch, Chris. "Jimmy Page: Paganini of the Seventies." *Melody Maker*, February 1970.

———. "Jimmy Page: The Power and the Glory." *Melody Maker*, March 1974.

———. *Led Zeppelin: Dazed and Confused.* London: Carlton, 1998.

———. *Peter Grant: The Man Who Led Zeppelin.* London: Omnibus, 2002.

Williams, Mark. Review of Led Zeppelin. *International Times*, 1969.

Williamson, Nigel. "Good Times . . . Bad Times: Robert Plant." *Uncut*, May 2005.

———. "'Forget the Myths': Jimmy Page." *Uncut*, May 2005.

Yorke, Ritchie. *Led Zeppelin: The Definitive Biography.* London: Virgin, 1993.

———. "Zeppelin Take the States by Storm." *New Musical Express*, May 1973.